PROGRESS OF A MODERN PILGRIM

My Life as an Ambassador of Faith and Film

DAVID SULLIVAN

malcolm down

PUBLISHING

WHAT OTHERS ARE SAYING...

'The map of someone's life always leads in unexpected directions. Reading *Progress of a Modern Pilgrim – My Life as an Ambassador of Faith & Film* is a reminder of how much is planned, and how much more is unplanned. David Sullivan has led a remarkable life, and been on the front lines of how technology has changed the way Christians engage with the world. His life is a testimony that to be a witness today means to speak the language of media, which is the language of the culture. It's a fascinating story, and one that needs to be told.'
Phil Cooke, filmmaker, media consultant, and author of Unique: Telling Your Story in the Age of Brands and Social Media

'David Sullivan is a gracious, thoughtful and inspired media ambassador of faith and film. He has integrity and wit. I commend him.'
Dr Ted Baehr, publisher of Movieguide

'I hope that many hearts will be touched by this wonderful record of one extraordinary man's journey with God.'
Dr Young Hoon Lee, Senior Pastor, Yoido Full Gospel Church (the world's largest church)

'Every time I chat with David I'm encouraged by his passion for Jesus and his desire to share the good news with the world. I'm also amazed at how many wonderful, providential and crazy situations he manages to find himself in. This book reads, appropriately given David's career path, like the plot of a film. It's an exciting invitation to follow David as he follows Christ.'
Andy Croft, Senior Pastor, Soul Survivor

PROGRESS OF A MODERN PILGRIM

'I have known David Sullivan for many years now and have been staggered by his amazing range of knowledge of Christian activity across the globe and in particular for what he has achieved in going to North Korea as a practising Christian Evangelist. I served with the United Nations in the Korean War as a twenty year old and know what it is like to fight in that far away country and how grateful the people of South Korea are for what servicemen and women did to bring about peace. Since then it is people like David who have done so much for so long to bring better relations between the two halves of this greatly divided country.'
Gospatric Home, Founder & Honorary President – The Christian Resources Exhibition

'I wish David every success with his amazing new book and the journey that he has taken. David is truly a modern day "ambassador of faith and film" – his book shows this.'
Sam Childers, Machine Gun Preacher

4

DEDICATION

Since my life has been so filled with so many events, meetings, projects, activities and so on it is impossible to include just a few thank yous for those who have input so much into my life. I had originally included one dedication for each chapter, but it was felt that it would be better to help the flow to place them in one entire section – so here goes:

CHAPTER 1: This chapter is dedicated to my parents, who sacrificed their time, their energy, their prayer, their entire life and finances to help my sister and I spread the gospel of Jesus Christ throughout the world.

CHAPTER 2: I would like to dedicate this chapter to my sister, Maria, who has, throughout her life, served the Lord on so many difficult mission fields in this world – labouring through blood, sweat and tears to bring the gospel to the unreached. She has been both an example and an inspiration to me and to my life and ministry.

CHAPTER 3: I dedicate to my Old Testament professor, Dr Marvin Wilson, who has always loved his students with the agape love of God, and instilled in me a love of the original Hebrew language of the Old Covenant and a love for the land of Israel and the Jewish people.

CHAPTER 4: I would like to dedicate this chapter to the principal and president of the Christian school that I attended – from kindergarten until graduation from high school – Rev Mahlon and Cecile Ameigh, long since passed onto their heavenly reward.

CHAPTER 5: This chapter is dedicated to my co-workers and church leaders, Ray and Diane Tambaschi, and their son Josh, who have tirelessly and sacrificially assisted in praying and sowing into this work for decades so that the world might know Jesus!

CHAPTER 6: This chapter is dedicated to a man I am privileged to call a friend and co-worker in the kingdom – Dr Young Hoon Lee – senior pastor of the world's largest church, Yoido Full Gospel Church in Seoul, South Korea. He is one of the most humble men of God that I have ever met, has been a friend through thick and thin and always had time for fellowship and prayer with me – oftentimes delaying his flight for an important trip to be with me.

CHAPTER 7: This chapter is dedicated to George Verwer, founder of Operation Mobilisation and the Logos Hope ship ministry – a good friend who has, more than any other person, encouraged our DVD production and programmes and shared them all across the globe – by the tens of thousands!

CHAPTER 8: This chapter is dedicated to Dr Luis Palau, who graciously opened his heart and his work for us to help to reach the people of China. His humility and time to fellowship with me has also inspired me.

CHAPTER 9: To my wonderful wife and children that have been such an inspiration and rock through the good times and through the bad. Because of the sensitivity of the countries that I work in, and for their security, I have left their story out – for the moment.

CHAPTER 10: This chapter is dedicated to Ed and Sherry Benish, who had the vision, courage and faith to pioneer national pastors and leaders conferences, starting in Cambodia, by faith and at no cost to the workers, to pour Jesus into us and refreshing times into the hearts of thousands.

CHAPTER 11: This chapter is dedicated to evangelist Dr James Sideras, who opened doors of ministry and gave of himself for me to share with the pastors and leaders in Cyprus.

CHAPTER 12: This chapter is dedicated to the many believers who serve the Lord in the closed countries and sectors of this world, many whom I have had the privilege to meet face-to-face, tirelessly serving their Lord and Saviour in prisons, labour camps and in secret.

CHAPTER 13: This chapter is dedicated to good friend, ambassador for Christ, world champion boxer and bold senator of the nation of the Philippines, Manny Pacquiao. Thank you for opening your home and heart and life to me.

CHAPTER 14: This chapter is dedicated to author A.J. Jacobs, who taught me more about The Bible in his book The Year of Living Biblically (Arrow, 2009) than almost any other person on earth. He has also taken the time for us to correspond and get to know more about each other. His developing fame also in TV and film shows how his promotion of God's Word has also promoted him.

CHAPTER 15: I dedicate this chapter to the great men and women of God most of whom I have never met, yet have been such an inspiration to my life –

Jim Elliot and the five martyred missionaries

Billy Graham and his team

Jack Wyrtzen for being what I would call 'an open minded 'fundamentalist', leading such a dynamic ministry and being a friend

St Augustine, who wrote so lovingly of his life with God

The pioneer doctors and workers who wrote their amazing autobiographies of their lives that challenged me as a boy

Charles Spurgeon, who took London by storm from his pulpits

George Müller, who believed God in order to care for the weak and neglected

Martin Luther, who took a raging bull by the horns and nailed his future to a door in Germany

C.S. Lewis, whose writing I have fallen in love with again by befriending his stepson

Corrie ten Boom, who is probably my number one 'most missed interviewee' that I would love to have filmed – on earth.

CONTENTS

CONTENTS

FOREWORD

There are many marks of God's providence and guidance in the life of a person who devoted himself to God. Even though he does not understand the meaning of what happened to him in a particular moment, it eventually turns out that God was present in every occasion of his life.

Reading his truly remarkable autobiography, I could find these marks of God in the life of David Sullivan. As the leader of Principles TV & HFC International, David Sullivan has unmistakable traces of God's providence in his ministry of raising and dispatching Christian leaders all over the world. Progress of a Modern Pilgrim is a vivid portrait of these divine touches.

David Sullivan was blessed with the heritage of faith passed on by his parents. He became God's servant through the love, devotion and prayer of his family. There have been many divine appointments for him to meet people he needed to meet. His life's journey has often included unexpected turns, but God has faithfully guided his life all along this incredible journey.

I believe the blessing David Sullivan has experienced is not automatically given to all the children of God. David Sullivan has walked with God with an attitude of obeying whatever God calls him to do without hesitation. He has also maintained the attitude of absolute positivity and absolute thanksgiving. If one serves the Lord as David Sullivan did, I believe that one will also experience the wonderful blessing David Sullivan has enjoyed.

I hope that many hearts will be touched by this wonderful record of one extraordinary man's journey with God.

Young Hoon Lee
Senior Pastor
Yoido Full Gospel Church

INTRODUCTION

At approximately 2am the fear crept over me like the icy hand of a skeleton, and yet here I was perspiring with such a heavy sweat that it soaked me through. I was not yet in the hands of a totalitarian regime – like I would be in the distant future. I was not even camping with just a mosquito net in the Brazilian jungles, with just a few young men next to the Amazon River – like I would be in the future. I was in a fully furnished room of a deserted wing of a hospital in England. I was fourteen years old and my sister, a nurse, and I were travelling across the British Isles – meeting some of our pen friends (fashionable in that day – 1967) along the way.

I was alone on the uninhabited wing – my sister was staying in a different wing with some of her nurse friends. I was almost deathly afraid of the dark, of the unknown and of unfamiliar surroundings. I could not sleep in a room without some sort of a light on. Often the fear would keep me awake half the night and then I would just fall asleep from the exhaustion and the energy expended by my all-encompassing phobia.

From a very young age, I was extremely fearful of being alone and in the dark – two phobias that might be common for a toddler but oh-so-very-strange in a teen.

Writing this might seem out of place in an autobiography of a life with so many, many contrasts to it. Yet, to think back now on the fears that kept the lights on and my mind wrapped up in a darkness of the unknown, it almost seems like the life of another person. From swimming in the creature-inhabited Amazon River to stumbling upon a South American revolution, to a nation whose people and sites are a closely guarded secret, it would seem unfeasible to think that this was the same person in the same lifetime.

I do not know what it was that eventually broke me of this fear. I wish I did, because then I could help others trapped in this same icy grip. Visiting my sister in 1969 in the Amazon jungles with the Yanomami Indians, whom she assisted medically and spiritually, might have seriously helped. All of the males, about ten of us, along with some Yanomami guides, slept by the Amazon in a hammock and a mosquito net for a full week. Undoubtedly wild animals nosed around us, but somehow I went to sleep right away. We swam in order to fully bathe and clean off the humidity-encrusted layers of dirt and perspiration. We knew there were anaconda and piranha in the water, and tarantulas, poisonous snakes and cheetahs on the edge of it. That was the chance we took for this brief respite from the heat.

Whatever it was, the fear left and, later in life, I faced some of the greatest unknowns that almost any human being could ever face – spending time in North Korea, China, Cambodia, and other places that would bring fear to the heart of anyone – even those who did not have such phobias. God did a great work in my mind, my heart and my life.

Writing this book has been a lot like the journey of my life of faith. It started out, probably in my youth, when I thought that my life might make an interesting book – even at that stage. Then in an interview and meeting with an Anglican bishop – David Pytches – he urged me to get this book done. Chapters were written on many of my worldwide missionary journeys – to China, South Korea, North Korea. The rewrite happened in hotel rooms in Cyprus, Lebanon, and then Ethiopia more recently. As each week passed, so many events and open doors from God made me think about adding another few paragraphs and then a chapter. From this I can then clearly say that it was God, busily writing my life with chapter and verse upon my heart – and *through* me, as I like to say, not just *to* me!

I sometimes feel like I have lived a lifetime of lifetimes. My journey in the Lord has taken so many twists and turns. When I thought that I was going into a life of Hollywood excitement, I was called into the pastorate. After thirty years of the pastorate, the Lord led me in the direction of film and TV production, and then connection with Hollywood, Wall Street, Bond Street and so many other sectors. In the midst of that God opened doors, at the same time, to begin working in such places as China, North Korea and Cambodia!

I love the quote that is attributed to D.L. Moody: 'The world has yet to see what God can do with a man fully surrendered to Him.' That is such a challenge, as having a level of dedication to Him has opened so many unusual doors of utterance. I try not to look at my ability because I believe that God looks more at our availability. I believe that if you believe great things from God, you can attempt and expect great things from God. William Carey said similar words.

Yet, on the other hand, one thing that I have been telling the leaders that I am privileged to share with around the world is that everything we do is *not* the great things. It's the least things. In His hands, God makes them great.

All my life has been a series of footprints along the way. On one of my trips in China, I felt led to leave the hotel late at night. I sensed, 'Turn left. Turn right. Go up these stairs. Go into this room.' There I was in a smoky, noisy room filled with about 100 young Chinese smoking, drinking and dancing. I prayed for them.

A few hours later I questioned God, 'What was that all about?' I felt God answer me 'Do you realise that you are the *only* person who has *ever* prayed for these young people?' At that moment I felt that wherever God leads my steps, sometimes I won't know until eternity the reason behind those actions – but God's will is being done! Obedience is greater than sacrifice (see 1 Samuel 15:22).

Some might look at a pathway that has gone from teaching to pastoring to evangelising to church planting to media person to producing to pioneering as a winding path but, like the threads under the tapestry that Corrie ten Boom would always show when she shared her testimony of being miraculously released from a Nazi concentration camp, we see the underside but God sees the upper.

I believe that a life that is filled with *things* is a failure. I am so thankful to God that my own life has been more filled with people than things. They are people with names you would *never* know – our own leaders who build the churches, put on the seminars, carry the cameras and fold the newsletters. Then there are the hundreds of household names that God has allowed me to have everything from a cup of tea to a lifetime of friendship with – people such as Dr David Yonggi Cho, Dr. Young Hoon Lee, Joyce Meyer, General Sir Richard Dannatt, George Verwer, Loren Cunningham, Jackie Pullinger, Peter Buffett, Graham Kendrick, The Newsboys, Lord David Puttnam, Lord George Carey, Lord David Alton, Baroness Caroline Cox, Douglas Gresham, Anne Graham Lotz, Brother Andrew, Brother Yun – and hundreds of others. They are a rich tapestry.

I started working in China over eleven years ago, when it

was still economically up and coming. Today it is vying for the pole position of world economy. This, which I had previously envisioned as the end of this book in my first draft, is more almost a halfway point. China led to both Cambodia and North Korea. Cambodia and the meetings that I spoke at there, led to the Philippines which, it appears, will lead to another time of adventures of faith in Israel – probably my eighth trip there. Every turn of the corner seems to be just another uphill climb and a plateau into a time of ministry and new friendships in what, when I was growing up, were the far-flung corners of the globe. Often in church I would help to design posters for missionary conferences of great works done in these nations by visiting missionaries. I would hear their stories but never in a million years imagine that I would be meeting many of them and learning about their particular parts of the world – from so many perspectives.

People call me a 'networker', but I like to say that my life is full of very deep connections. Sometimes, when talking to others, I feel led to mention someone's name. I am not name-dropping, but trawling to see what the connection is with that particular person. Why have I mentioned *their* name in *this* conversation? Almost every time there is a connection there and God confirms His Word with signs following.

While some people are building empires, my own life's ambition has been to promote my Lord and Saviour any way that I can. If that means having coffee with one of the world's leading business people in Beijing or talking to a shoe-shine boy in Shanghai, that is what I am led to do. With every connection I share the miracles of what God is doing in my life and ministry. The stories come from a Paris catwalk or a British film set to a Chinese house church or a Cambodian connection. People listen intently and the stories inspire them to trust in God more, and in His leading their footsteps in faith.

Many people tell me that they would like to work with me. I explain that *security* is a word that in the physical realm, I do not know. One moment I might be called to film at the Cannes Film Festival and the next to a dangerous part of the world, and perhaps next to the Killing Fields to tell a particular story. It's not the life I saw for myself, but it is so much more worthwhile than what has been called 'a Monday to Friday kind of dying'. It's been literally decades since I walked into a new car showroom and ordered a car. Yet it has been decades since I've woken up in the morning and thought to myself, 'What *am* I going to do with myself and my life today?'

People quite often ask me to tell them what my favourite country is, or favourite person that I have interviewed. That is so difficult to do. Although I do get to see snippets of nations, I am quite often peering through the viewfinder of a camera, living life through an electronic array of screens and monitors. From time to time I look back and remember watching a small fisherman's boat glide across the Mekong River in Phnom Penh. I stopped briefly for lunch at the Foreign Correspondents Club, where the history of what once was hits you like the cool breeze wafting through the open windows overlooking everyday life in this unique city. That memory is fleeting, pushed out by the memory of the crunching sound made, just a few miles away, walking onto the bones of the victims of the Killing Fields, freshly surfacing after the spring rains and flooding. This memory then brings me back to the same action, but this time walking on the ash-filled dirt of Auschwitz and Birkenau, a place where, it is said, it is impossible to *not* walk on the ashes of the thousands of Jews who were murdered there.

INTRODUCTION

In my years of ministry and documenting of these various places, I am sometimes awed at the beauty of God's creation but, in the next step, am grieved by man's inhumanity to man in some of those most beautiful locations. Being in many ways a documenter of God's planet, I must mix together these two worlds, then write a script and film, a reaction to what I see and what I understand.

In grappling in my heart and mind the difference between the missionaries I met as a child and then a teen and their work, and what we have been given in the twenty-first century to be able to accomplish the same goal – I find that today's missionaries are also visionaries as well as involved in media and 'good works'. Today's Middle Eastern countries do not welcome their arms to Christian hospitals and saintly nurses as they once did. It is indeed a day and age when we must be wise as serpents and harmless as doves (see Matthew 10:16). There are some nations that I step foot into that I cannot be a card-carrying Christian, have religious feelings, or even admit to knowing my way around a broadcast camera. In those places I am merely a tourist, enthusiastically imbibing the culture and asking an unusual number of questions to suss out the situation. In twentieth-century America we were sure that missions would be practised until the return of Jesus Christ! That is not the case any longer.

Unlike many young people today, caught up in the media craze and video addiction I, like others of my generation, was weaned and raised next to a pile of books and read to by my mother, or by myself. They challenged my thinking and my imagination, and included the usual British and American classics – the works of Charles Dickens and Samuel Langhorne Clemens – Mark Twain. In the cinema of my imagination, each boyhood summer I would reread Tom Sawyer and float down the mighty Mississippi. I would be dodging criminals on the streets of Dickensian London. Added to this were the great missionary classics that reflected the visitors to our home, with their tales of being a doctor in Africa, nursing in Asia and teaching the children of South America. When it came to the printed word, I believe that for some time our home received the daily local newspaper. Yet most of my life was without any kind of political controversy and upheavals throughout the world. We knew that the world was in need, not because of who was in power, but because so many rejected the plan laid down in God's Word for humankind. Today that might seem like a simplistic view of the world, but maybe that is what is missing in our visual-hungry society!

My thoughts and prayers and hopes are that in my life's story, and some snippets from it, that people will be encouraged in the same way that they have been when I have shared with people one-to-one. People tell me, 'I wish the exciting things that happen to you would happen to me.' I tell them that we serve the same God and that He wants to use everyone.

I used to pray, while in China, 'God, please order my footsteps today.' I would see phenomenal things happen. Then I realised that I could pray the same thing in the country in which I live. Guess what? The same miraculous things started happening.

I remember mentioning this to my wife in the car once and I said, 'I think that God is about to do something for His glory in the next few hours.' We went about our routine and nothing seemed to happen. I went to fill up my car with fuel and a woman knocked on my window and asked me to help her with her jump leads. Maybe *that* was what God was saying. Or maybe He just wanted to know if I was still available to Him.

I love this exciting Christian life. I now feel that every one of my footsteps matters to God and He wants to lead these funny feet into and across the map called 'His Will'. I pray that this is your journey and your testimony too!

CHAPTER 1
The Early Years
(1952-70)

Only one life,
'twill soon be passed.
Only what's done for Christ
will last.
(C.T. Studd, 1860–1931)

(This poem was in place on the visor in all of my father's cars
through the years.)

My generation has been called the baby boomer generation. Following World War Two, so many families felt secure in a lasting peace, finally, that they decided to start a family or add to their family by having another child. Or maybe it was the realisation that life is temporary and investing in children instead of belongings was a better way of life. Whatever the reason – there are a lot of us. Many of us are coming into retirement age, and the generation that followed that was so very careful *not* to reproduce is shouldering the burden of the rest of us!

In understanding what had made me, me – I have always been interested in that age old debate – Nature versus Nurture. Looking back to my birth, infancy and boyhood, you can see the influences of both. To me the scales are balanced, and the jury is still out. There are many things that I can contribute to my Christian upbringing – strict, but not overly, discipline, living two decades after the Great Depression. Yet, on the other hand, an interest in media and telling my story around the world had no family background.

Train up a child in the way he should go, and when he is old he will not depart from it.
(Proverbs 22:6, RSV)

That was a scripture heard in our house quite often – especially when I would question why my parents were so seemingly strict while other parents at church seemed to let their children freestyle throughout their upbringing. I would often be taken out of the church service and receive a stern talking-to by my mother. Occasionally there was the spanking which I tended to block out of my memory, not because of the cruelty of it, but the embarrassment. Many of the other children my age never received such and, I believe, suffered later on in life with not having limits imposed at a very early age.

I understand the fascination that people today might have in living through the 1950s. It was an exciting era but we did not know that at the time. It was just life. I can watch a collecting TV show such as *American Pickers* and every item, every toy, every jukebox brings back nostalgic memories which flood my mind and emotions. This time was simple and unencumbered with technology and corruption. We did not know what we lacked. I grew up in what today would be considered a degree of poverty. Yet we wanted for nothing. It was similar to when I was in Carnaby Street in London in 1967. It was *just* London and I was visiting it for the first time. I didn't know that I was in the middle of cultural and music history as The Beatles' songs played in the shops and Mary Quant's fashion was everywhere.

But I get ahead of myself.

My very first memory stems from a story that my mother used to tell people for years. After being born on a mild Thursday December day in 1952, it was not the warmth and security of our home that I saw first, but a fledgling Christian school. My parents were good friends with the headmistress and president – a strict husband and wife team who had previously pastored the local Baptist church that my mother and father attended. My mother felt it appropriate for her new bundle of joy to see and be seen in this new-ish spiritual venture for America, and revolutionary for Roman Catholic Massachusetts.

Little did they know that the school and I would grow up together. Each year of my life, a new grade was added to it. This made it possible for me to graduate in 1970 from that Christian school just before a major illness hit the president, a takeover by the board of directors, and the contraction and eventual demise of my beloved scholastic institution. Just before the sale of my much-remembered school building, I was allowed to go through it and take away any of the books scattered aimlessly throughout – small mementos that would bring back so many memories, good and bad. It was one of the saddest experiences of my life, going through the empty carcass, chairs and books thrown around, and to remember so many good times, so many growing times echoing on the walls of my memory. Without the young men and young women, it was actually cold and sterile. In its early years, the building had been a Jewish institution of higher learning. The Star of David would turn up in the most unusual locations, such as cupboards and mosaics on the ground outside. It is quite important to know why this school was such a miracle.

The city of Fall River, Massachusetts used to be a lifeline – the manpower of the production industry for America. Its many mills spewed out cotton thread, wire, shoes, tyres and innumerable numbers of items important for an America about to redefine itself – by its highways and roads. Eventually the Southern part of the US and then, later, locations overseas, would slowly drain that lifeblood from the livelihoods of tens of thousands of working-class men and women who depended on the buildings characterised by giant chimney stacks and smoke. A metropolis of about 100,000 people, it was just like New York City to me.

Fall River, though, in my early years, was known mostly for a young lady, a Christian, who loved church and being a member of her church's youth group. Her name was Lizzie Borden. I would often pass her house and view the items from her world-renowned trial at the local museum. The popular rhyme of the day went:

Lizzie Borden took an axe
And gave her mother forty whacks.
When she saw what she had done,
She gave her father forty-one.
(anonymous)

You can imagine how gruesome this was in the days when no such mainstream horror films or, perish the thought, TV programmes were aired. Oddly enough, I understand that there has been, in recent years, a Lizzie Borden TV series – quite tame, I would imagine, being placed side by side with vampires and tales of zombies.

The results of the trial found the young girl innocent, and it has gone down in history as one of the most controversial verdicts in American legal history. Charming! I remember being on the NBC Television Network backstage tour at Rockefeller Center in New York City when I was asked where I was from, as a child of thirteen.

'Fall River,' I said.

'Oh,' came the reply, 'the city of Lizzie Borden.'

Just a few weeks ago, someone sent me an internet link to a photo that showed that Lizzie Borden's house, once the location of a printing shop in later years, was now a very popular Bed and Breakfast! I would never have imagined that happening in my younger days.

This gruesome infamy was probably only part of the reason for my burning desire to go beyond the borders of that city, beyond Somerset and Dighton and Tiverton – the most desirous of suburbs – to an interesting place with more culture, scenery and prospects for fulfilling work. Maybe the desire was there to fulfil my interests in TV, radio and film – though never having been in a cinema in my life!

Spiritually, the city was 99 44/100 per cent Roman Catholic, or at least that is what people said. We are talking about pre-Vatican II Roman Catholicism. Here, many hours on Fridays were spent buying fish and chips. It was like standing in line at the Vatican waiting to see the Sistine Chapel. Meat was anathema on a Friday because 'Jesus died on a Friday' and the entire Roman Catholic world had to suffer with Him. This profited the fish sellers and the fish and chip trade immensely. For us *Protestants* it meant huge lines of people if you decided to have this special treat on *that* day of the week!

Being a Protestant in that world meant that one was like a salmon swimming upriver. The RC churches in our city were actually cathedrals – some of the most renowned in New

England. They featured huge paintings, murals and artwork and statues that Catholics from across America would come to see. I rarely looked inside these buildings. Finally, after some burned down and others were knocked down to create more modern places of worship, I did learn to appreciate the beauty that had been right under my nose.

My father had been a Roman Catholic, but when he met my mother, a committed Christian, he turned his life over to Jesus Christ – or, as some put it, *walked down the aisle*. My mother became a deaconess in our local Baptist church and my father a deacon. Women could not hold influential roles so her 'job function' was to help with setting out the monthly communion, washing the communion dishes and helping with the robes after people were baptised by immersion in water.

In many ways I loved and still miss many aspects of Fall River, not having been back for decades, because it was a miniature copy of the world. There was a Chinese section, a Russian section, a Jewish section, an Italian section, a Polish section – and so on. I was born and brought up in the Irish area, nicknamed Corky Row. My father's side of the family were from Ireland and I assume this is why our family had settled in this area. We never knew that we were poor or that that was even a *class* as such. We were happy, had three meals a day and a roof over our heads.

One of the greatest joys I had was when, in the summer, people would hang around outside, chatting about things in many languages, and sometimes strum a guitar, singing national or folk songs. You do not see that happen very much nowadays, anywhere. Our neighbourhood was a tiny bit of the Emerald Isle right there in America. Later the city became, while growing up, about 90 per cent plus Portuguese, as that whole area of New England did. A large number of Fado clubs sprang up, bringing the culture of this music and dance to America. My mother's side of the family was Portuguese, but sadly, I did not get to know and understand the culture at that time.

With this rich multicultural background, it is no wonder that I sensed the calling of God to reach the far corners of the globe with missionary work and media and go into countries that few have ever ventured into – that, and probably the fact that my parents would invite missionaries into our home to tell of their adventures, after showing their slides about their work in the church services. In a way, our home was a port of call for those needing a place to stay or to visit. At Christmastime and Thanksgiving we often had sailors come to our house for a meal from nearby Newport, Rhode Island (back then one of the largest US Navy bases in the world) – away from home for these important celebrations.

When my mother began to teach at that same Christian school that I visited as a baby, she also came into contact with people from other nations. She tried their recipes, learned some of their language and helped them to feel at home in America. She celebrated their birthdays with special parties during school time and befriended those without husbands. I still remember having 'Swedish Christmas stollen' and 'Russian Tea Cookies' (which I later discovered no Russians had ever had and actually resembled Greek Easter cookies).

If my sister – who was eleven years older than me – was home from nursing school, she would play our family piano (complete with the rolls of a pianola which made us appear as though we were accomplished musicians) – especially at Christmas or Thanksgiving; sometimes she would play her accordion or trumpet. My cousins, on my mother's side of the family, David and Raymond and little Ruthie, would come by for evenings of music where the three of them, with my sister, would put on impromptu concerts. We even went to the nearby amusement park, Lincoln Park, and made our own little 45rpm record of a few Christian songs – I kept it for years. Almost all the songs we sang were Christians songs – many had just been written in the 1950s for growing American churches and large crusades such as Billy Graham's. Music was such a big part of my life – music and travel and church and family.

The subject of travel would be appropriate to mention here as America in the 1950s and 1960s was in love with travel. Travel on the highways, as the new interstates connected the nation, where you could go from Boston to Los Angeles without ever passing through a single city. Driving at speeds of 55–65mph meant that the entire nation – east to west – could, technically, be covered in seventy-two hours of driving non-stop. My father, a couple of times, drove us from Massachusetts to Chicago in twenty-four hours – with a brief respite at a motel, a new kind of hotel where you could park right next to the room.

Foreign travel, on the other hand, was the subject of romantic films. Every major Hollywood movie took place in at least one European capital where the champagne, luxury hotels and unusual flashy cars would be featured. The planes were designed to look like spaceships, as space travel was all the rage.

In the 1950s in America, you bought car and life insurance and paid for it in person. Every month my father would visit our insurance agency to pay his $4.95 or whatever and wait for the hand-written receipt. Eventually the insurance agent had the brilliant idea of also handling travel tickets – flights, trains and the like. This captured my imagination. I would take a copy of the free brochures beautifully showing the exotic destinations which one could *fly* to! This part of the company's business grew so much that a man and then his wife were employed to run the Travel Agency. I would read articles about travel and the sites around the world and the cheapest way to get there. One of the most popular books at the time was *Europe on $5 a Day*. My personal copy of it was dog-eared and heavily underlined. Eventually Americana Travel, as the agency was called, moved to their own premises and I was treated as a VIP guest at the opening. I often discussed the possibility of my becoming a travel agent on graduation from college. Through the years I would go to buy a flight ticket or tour and explain the various codes and limitations of it with the couple, who often had not yet even heard about these things.

Eventually my bedroom had a few of the promotional items in it – a three-foot Eiffel Tower was one of my proudest acquisitions! After our family went to New York City I took an old Timex watch display cabinet and made it into a Museum of New York City. Items in it included a Chinese fortune cookie from China Town – something not yet seen in the outback of Massachusetts. Travel was a passion of mine, but Christianity was still the centre of my life and being. When I was small, every night my mother would read a Bible story to me and so, at the young age of six, I realised that, as my friend Dr Luis Palau says, 'God has no grandchildren. Each generation must receive – or reject – Jesus Christ for themselves.' I realised that I needed to have a personal relationship with and faith in Jesus Christ for myself.

A Christian youth and children's camp in what we called upper New York State – Word of Life – sent some of their team from the Word of Life Ranch to our church to hold a children's rally. An invitation was given at the end of the programme to receive Jesus. I very cautiously thought about it and then walked down that aisle. I always look back on that time as my 'Damascus

Road' moment. Although I had no life of crime, grand theft or murders to turn from, I received what God offered me through Jesus on the cross – the opportunity to become a child of God. That moment so affected me that the next day I was out with some of the neighbour boys sharing the gospel and asking them if they would like to pray to become a Christian. My bicycle had a mirror which, on the reverse, said, 'Ye Must Be Born Again!' Later, at the age of twelve, I followed the example of Jesus and was baptised as a believer by immersion in that same little Baptist church.

I grew spiritually but even faster physically. After having a number of years of birthday parties – *all boys* – as my mother emphasised, she started to look at celebrations from different angles. I think the kicker was my twelfth birthday when fifteen to twenty of us boys gathered in a small apartment (called a tenement – made for factory workers and six tenements to a building/block) for a birthday celebration. I vividly remember the astronauts on the cake – a favourite theme of mine. Very politically incorrectly we decided that we wanted to play hide-and-seek in the apartment with all of these boys including a Middle Eastern boy who was *blind!* We never thought of him as different because of any handicap, and always included him in everything – even watching TV. The crashes and bangs lasted, for my parents, for what must have been an eternity. That was the last birthday party I had like that.

I came up with the idea of my thirteenth birthday being a weekend in New York City with, because it was my *big birthday*, tickets to the ballet – *The Nutcracker* (being Christmastime) at the newly built Lincoln Center. We enjoyed it immensely and even took the backstage tour of the opulent facilities that had just been built at immense cost.

One day, while we were walking down the street in Manhattan, I was given some tickets for us to attend a TV taping at the NBC Studios next to Radio City Music Hall at Rockefeller Center. Watching the cameras and taking notes about what everybody did, I then never stopped writing for tickets for our special annual December weekend in New York City. Sometimes I met some of the 'celebrity contestants' such as Alan Young, 'Wilbur' in the *Mr Ed* TV show about a talking horse.

So there you have it – all the ingredients for a budding career in media, which at that stage was still on black and white TV! No satellites, streaming, digital or 3D anything. Just lots of fun and learning. I can even remember creating a science project on Telstar – the satellite launched into space in 1962 that enabled TV transmissions and telephone calls worldwide. I was enamoured of everything media.

My interest also connected with the emerging American space programme. I had posters on my walls of the seven original astronauts. For some reason both the areas of space exploration and media production were way out there in my mind! They were indications that a modern age was upon us that would open up things and events that were unimaginable at that time. We *never* would have imagined TV on a portable phone that you could place in your pocket. Even the TV space-age cartoon show *The Jetsons* was not that advanced with their storylines!

Although space and media were my twin thrills in life, space exploration was not anything I could envisage doing in the near future. Media, however, was another story. When I became a teen, I had a chance to spend a few years being the 'producer' of another (Baptist) church's live radio programme. My whole job entailed phoning the radio station that we were airing on to get a time check , synchronising our watches and then pressing the red button when we were five minutes from air and then the green when we went live (or was it the other way around?). The only problem was that one Sunday morning a baseball game was running over and the pastor never received his green light. I can just imagine his bewilderment of not knowing if he was On Air or whether the teenager had fallen asleep backstage!

My school was not that large. A Christian school in a parochial school city, its classes were quite small – especially as the years advanced and more and more parents and students wanted the large range of activities that larger high schools offered. I did, however, get to be on a basketball team which had away games in other parts of New England. By the time I graduated from high school in 1970 there was only one other student in the class – and we were the very last class to graduate from that school. The other student was the son of a pastor and went into the pastorate himself. We would communicate infrequently and get together every five years or so. The last I heard was that he had died of a disease a number of years ago in Florida.

In its heyday it was decided that a good school needed a yearbook. The problem was that to pay for a yearbook the school needed a hard-hitting sales team. Thus we, the students, were enrolled, and a contest created to see who would sell the most yearbooks. I won the first year quite easily. Many kids thought it was because my mother was a teacher in one of the school's nursery classes, as well as a personal friend of the headmistress. She was the driving force behind me but, not sounding boastful, it was all my blood, sweat and tears that brought the numbers.

The second year the niece of the headmistress, who had suddenly appeared on the scene, decided that she was going to win. I had to redouble my efforts, but still won. My mother's strategy for me was to always keep them guessing. I would bring in dribs and drabs of sales until the very last day. It was then that I would bring in one or two $100 bills (that few people had ever seen in their life). The first couple of years that photo of me handing over the $100 bill appeared in the yearbook. The third year they decided that they had had enough of me winning, so they decided to add yearbook advertising sales with actual yearbook sales to make it 'fairer'. Yes, I won again. I spent months going through our city of 100,000 people and its businesses getting advertising space as well as selling the yearbook.

The next year they had really had enough of my constant winning. It was decided that the winning class would have a pizza party for winning. Everyone thought that it was a 'sure thing' for our class but, again, I tried to keep them guessing until the last whistle. *That* was the final year of the yearbook, for some reason!

My 'sales experience' and 'career' extended beyond school time. I was always an industrious young man – carrying a briefcase with me at all times. I remember a photo of me going into hospital at five or six years of age, and there was my 'Mickey Mouse' briefcase.

When I became a teen I was a busy entrepreneur. I had a paper round, which my father would help me with, delivering hundreds of newspapers every morning, from 5am to 6am. At six we would finish and my father would drive me to the house of a nurse, a co-worker of my sister, to babysit she and her husband's two children (who spent most of the time sleeping). Then at eight I would go to school. After school I had a 'Grit' (rural America) newspaper route, sold Christmas and greetings cards and, at Christmastime, worked 4–8pm or later ringing the bell outside of department stores for the Salvation Army, making the minimum wage. In my other time (what was left), I completed my schoolwork and studies.

I was what you would call an average student, but only because I did not really apply myself to my studies. I was interested in TV and film and reading about what was happening in the world around me and further afield. Years later I learned that because of the high level of academics in our school, the 'average' grades that I was getting were actually quite high compared with the grading in other schools. My C level grade would actually have been a high B or A, even. I found this high bar of success did seem to push me a bit harder, which was good for me.

In 1967 I decided that I would go with my sister to London for the amazing price of $293! My sister had studied nursing in Chicago after graduating from high school, and then did a midwifery course with the Frontier Nursing Service in rural Kentucky and a bachelor's degree in Rhode Island. She always seemed to be away, so it was a good chance for us to spend three weeks together exploring a new country – or countries.

Both she and I had a pen friend in England, so we included a visit to meet them in our tour. In the twenty-one days we visited England, Ireland (where I kissed the Blarney Stone. Can you tell?) and Wales – as well as spending some time in London. Youth hostels back then were great for young people and a cheap and safe place to stay. We visited Windsor Castle (where we stayed at a youth hostel), Stratford-upon-Avon, Edinburgh Castle and our family's old homestead in Cork, Ireland (not the house, just the area). I fell in love with the people of England and the whole pattern and pace of life. In 1967 many people used bicycles and, if you owned a car, for many families it was kept mainly for emergencies and used for a Sunday drive. The same appeared to be true when I returned in 1970, although the roads seemed to be getting busier!

The next summer, 1968, I used some of my finances to visit a school friend who had moved with his mother to Baton Rouge, Louisiana. His brother-in-law owned a French pastry shop. What an experience! His brother-in-law picked me up at the airport in an experimental Corvette Stingray that went up past 100mph (I won't say how far past it). After my time with them, from Louisiana I took a Greyhound Bus to Houston, Texas. My plan was to travel to Mexico City, but rioting during the summer there changed my plans – as did an awful experience in San Antonio, Texas.

Taking the bus to such a beautiful city as San Antonio with its beautiful boats and canal was an experience in itself. My plan was to visit the HemisFair 1968 – the World's Fair being held there that year. On the way to the fair site, I walked by a second-hand store with a Kodak Super 8mm movie camera and bought it for $10. That really changed my life as I was now able to make my own productions – and did, through the years, adding narration and sound on reel-to-reel tapes. My movie of the Cherry Blossom Festival in Washington, DC was probably my best work then and every one of my relatives was forced to sit through the fifteen-minute production.

Against better judgement, and probably against the leading of the Lord, I bought a ticket to the World's Fair late show concert with Jimmy Dean, a popular Country and Western singer. As the show finished at 11pm, I decided to walk to my hotel – only about one to two miles away. I had fallen in love with what I considered to be a very lovely city – with touches of Spanish architecture. Earlier in the day I had taken a boat ride along the canal running through the city and pictured it like a Tex-Mex version of Venice.

Every once in a while you would see what I would call a 'dodgy' character. Being right near the border with Mexico, I knew that it could be a bit of *Wild West* with drug trafficking, criminals who had come into the country illegally with other things on their mind than settling down and just generally dangerous people. Balancing that, though, were the genuine friendly and caring Texans whose hospitality is renowned across America – and the world!

I walked from the fair site past the canal and bridges and through the closed and sleepy city. I finally reached home stretch – the last street with any life in it, more closed shops, and then a large open space with car parking which could be a dangerous area at this time of night. But on the other side of that was my hotel. Everything had been uneventful and the clinging heat of the day gave way to a slightly cool breeze which, alone, could have encouraged me to let down my guard.

Within that last half mile of my hotel and about midnight, I noticed a man in a car slowly following me. It was an older car, typical of the ones driving around late at night – dark and unassuming. At this point I was definitely on my guard and starting to perspire as he followed me for too long and too closely. It wasn't a typical night drive, but one with some intended purpose. I was on the pavement and he stopped directly next to me. He stuck his head out of the car window to call me over. I saw his face – a slightly Mexican look to it and the air of someone pretending to be nice, but with hidden shadows in his nervous smile. That face will stick in my memory for as long as I live.

'Hey, son. Come here a second,' he said with a slight pretend Mexican accent. He followed me some more. 'Come here a second, son.' My eyes were darting back and forth looking for exits, alleyways or places that I could duck into where there would be people – witnesses.

Although illegal, I ducked into a bar that was open. Back then such places would always have a row of two or three payphones with a door that folded in half when opened but would close the whole world out. A small fan tried to cool off the claustrophobic area and sweat was now pouring down my face and soaking my shirt. Although I always repented of it, I had watched a number of murder mysteries and horror films (mild compared to ones today). I remembered what I would scream at the victims – what they should have done and where they should have gone. But this was not a film and I knew that I was in grave danger. Although I didn't think about it, I was only fifteen years old and thousands of miles away from home with no one that I knew anywhere around.

I telephoned 411 – directory enquiries – which you could do without inserting any money in the slot. I was shaking like a leaf and perspiring even more now. The operator could not 'just give me the number of any taxi company' as I had asked her to. I actually had to tell her which taxi company I wanted. 'But this is an emergency,' I pleaded. I would imagine that the operator wondered what kind of emergency a 'you should be in bed' teen could get up to!

I can remember that I finally ordered a taxi from the Acme taxi company (companies in the US used to randomly name their companies starting with the letter A so that they would appear first in the voluminous Yellow Pages of commercial phone numbers – in some cities two to three volumes long). I told the switchboard (that's what the receptionists used to be called at taxi companies) to ask the driver to come inside of the bar. He never appeared. The man chasing me, however, did come into the bar and watched me on the phone through the window in the phone booth. I also tried telephoning the police, but to no avail.

Finally the soft-hearted receptionist at my hotel helped me and sent over a security guard who actually came inside of the bar. He drove me back to the hotel and I could not thank him enough. The man following me had disappeared – at which point I don't know exactly. I was embarrassed that I could not prove I had been in danger, but thankful that it had passed and God had delivered me from peril and terror.

The next morning, after a sleepless night with the radio and lights on, I flew back home. This was the suggestion of my sister, whom I had called while she was working the night shift at the hospital when I arrived back at the hotel.

That event would have stayed to the back of mind except that a few years later, there was a news report of a man looking exactly like that same man who had followed me. It seems that he had kidnapped, raped and then buried the bodies of dozens and dozens of young teen boys in that particular area of Texas. Anyway, I thank God that He saved me that night.

CHAPTER 2
Brazil
(1969)

Wherever you are, be all there!
(Missionary martyr, Jim Elliot)

After hearing about the five missionaries who were martyred after attempting to reach a native tribe in South America, my sister, Maria, decided to dedicate herself to becoming a missionary nurse in Brazil.

She did become a missionary nurse, working for an inter-denominational Christian mission based in a beautiful leafy suburb of Philadelphia, Pennsylvania. Hundreds of people served worldwide as translators, doctors, nurses, teachers and other helpful professions. Some fields were so large that they were split up. For example, there was a great deal of city work in Brazil in places such as Belem (Portuguese for Bethlehem) and São Paolo. After a year of language study in Brazil, learning the Portuguese that our mother had spoken so fluently – not teaching it to us, she began to work in a smaller city in northern Brazil, Boa Vista.

Finally, in 1969 she started to serve as a missionary nurse with the 'prehistoric' Yanomami Indians in north-western Brazil, right next to the border with Venezuela. Her studies as a missionary nurse equipped her well for the varied life that she began to lead. She became a doctor, nurse, midwife, dentist, and even an undertaker!

In the Yanomami culture, women would be pregnant, sometimes having their baby right on the side of the trail. They would make a fire, have the baby, rest for a few minutes and then continue on their work or their walk to or from their village. If there were any type of complications with the birth, the woman was poorly equipped to help and in most cases, the baby would die.

My sister soon learned that in that culture, a boy baby is a joy and privilege, the breadwinner in the family. In my view, the women laboured just as hard by their work in the fields *and* taking care of the family. If a baby girl was born, often but not always they would be knocked over the head with a log and then left beside the pathway to die. My sister attempted to end this practice as much as she could, both practically and through re-education. Women would tell my sister that she would then need to take care of or adopt the child herself. However, they seemed to warm to the baby once it was born and allowed to live, and my sister adopted or took care of no child during her fifteen years of work there.

It was decided that I could go and visit her for her first summer in the jungles – June through August 1969. Flying with another missionary couple from Florida through the Caribbean, we landed at our first airport in South America on a dark and starless night on the outskirts of Georgetown, Guyana. It was actually in the middle of what we were told was a revolution. Hundreds of soldiers lined the runway with rifles pointing to the forests – and towards *us* – as the airport had been attacked the night before by rebels. Here I was now, a sixteen-year-old boy in the middle of a revolution, on my way to what was then the most primitive tribe in the world! Those early fears in life seemed to be crawling back to capture me once again.

After a couple of days in Guyana visiting the mission's HQ there, we finally arrived at Boa Vista, Brazil. It was a tiny town but gave a glimpse of this part of Brazil and a chance to acclimatise, temperature-wise and food-wise. With a diet of rice and beans – and mountains of it – it was a far cry from my normal seafood and meat back in Massachusetts. Most of the streets in the town were unpaved. I began to see that this would possibly be my last taste of things such as Coca-Cola and Pepsi-Cola – much needed in this summer heat!

After a few days we took a tiny 'jungle hopper' Cessna, flown by another Christian mission – Mission Aviation Fellowship. The group serviced every Christian mission that worked in the jungles. It was a shock to be able to fly for hours in a tiny plane over hundreds and hundreds of miles of just trees – dotted here and there with a clearing and usually a giant round house. This is what was called a *village*!

Each missionary organisation had their own particular priorities, regulations, theology and theory of how the indigenous Indians should be reached. Some started with good works projects and then led to telling Bible stories. Some had the notion that you needed to physically cover them up and then work with the people. (I sometimes think that this was more to do with the particular discomfort of the missionaries themselves than an actual command from God to replace their loincloths with trousers!)

The entire process of setting up a mission station is a very long, thought-out and prayed through process. The Hollywood film *End of the Spear* (scripted by a friend) tells the true story of five American missionaries who felt God's leading to contact a remote, untouched Indian group in South America. Their particular strategy was to first fly over the site of the village a number of times. Then they would drop down a basket with gifts for the Indians. Finally, when it seemed that the tribe was ready to receive them, they would land. On this particular occasion, all five missionary men were murdered by the Indians. The end of the story is, though, that one of the wives of the martyred men returned to the tribe and brought them the gospel of Jesus Christ – in essence, loving them into God's kingdom. The son of one of the missionaries helped to tell their story.

The mission station that I would be based at for ten weeks was the most newly established station. With this particular mission, a station consisted of a regulation size and length airstrip (mostly made of cut grass), and then small house-type buildings – grouped by families. In the case of singles, they would usually be housed in twos. In the more advanced mission stations there might be a school – even a store.

My sister was staying at the house of one of the mission families who were on furlough. A furlough used to take place every seven years and consisted of a year taken, mostly, to recuperate, readjust to Western life, and travel from church to church to bolster support, as well as working on any educational issues, if there were children of that age. This could consist of putting children into a normal (rather than home or boarding) school or looking at potential colleges for their future. (Most missionaries find this time exhausting. Thus some missionary agencies have started having mini-furloughs – three months off after just a few years' service.)

The house of the missionaries was roughly made, although quite plush by Indian standards. The area under the house was usually boarded off with a type of skirting around the home – to stop animals or interested Indians. Since they were quite resourceful (both Indians and animals), it usually did not do the trick! It was not unusual to find the floor slats (with gaps between the wood) having a set of eyes watching you as you dressed! Since modesty was not too much of a problem with the Yanomami, they always found it comical how much the 'white folk' went to great lengths to cover up! The typical Yanomami woman would have a string around her breasts (for beauty, *not* for modesty) and a small skirt to cover their private parts – just! The men had only a loincloth cover. Some Indian men merely had a string guard rather than a loincloth. Somehow, my young mind was kept pure!

Each of the houses had a door and a sort of reception area that was locked off from the main part of the house. The Indians could sit on the rows of benches surrounding the outer room and wait to be seen – or just watch the missionaries behind the cage! One of the most comical sights was when a female missionary would lose an earring through one of the cracks in the floor slats and, a week later, see one of the men having pierced it through his nose or ear! Then you would have a small kitchen, living/dining room and bedrooms. Outhouses were the order for the day, and it was always wise to check for tarantulas and snakes.

This newly built base was called by the Mission Surucucu – Portuguese for the bushmaster (poisonous) snake found throughout the area.

Each Sunday morning at Surucucu we would have a church service with all of the missionaries who were around at the time. With so many different families and situations, there seemed to be a constant flow in and out. Sometimes a family might need to take one of the children to a boarding school in Brazil or even to the States. That would take months as it would also include some speaking in churches to raise more much-needed support. Someone might need dentistry work and would have to wait for the next flight back. The plane was *the* lifeline for the missionaries. We had absolutely *no* connection with the outside world. When the pilot would fly back on a prearranged date, we would tune into a shortwave radio and hear his call – when he was about fifteen minutes away in his tiny plane. In later years I believe that two-way radios were installed to have constant contact with the outside world.

After the worship service we would walk to one of the Yanomami villages to spend time with the people, talk and listen to them and tell a Bible story. I must admit that even in my youth, I was not the most athletic person or into what would now be called extreme sports. Walking to a village would be a trek of anywhere from one to three hours – or further afield, an overnight journey. The trails were small paths, worn down by the feet of hundreds of Indians, and sometimes hard to see. Quite often one of our Indian guides would stop us mid-trek and show us a large snake or a petrifying tarantula. Their eyesight was quite remarkable. We would walk across logs (sometimes branches) laid out across streams or rivers. As almost everyone just sauntered across I would sit on the log and shimmy myself across – much to everyone's laughter – especially the Indians!

We were warned as we approached the village (actually just a large open-roofed, round building made with tree branches and leaves). The area just outside of each village was the village toilet! This was a breeding ground for small, nasty bugs. After each visit it was necessary to stop in the stream, take your shoes and socks off and thoroughly wash off these tiny insects. If you missed one – I would often miss six or more – they would start burrowing into your skin. The only remedy was to burn a safety pin, sterilising it, and then carefully cut around where the egg sack was thought to be and gingerly lift the contents of bug and eggs out of your skin. You can be sure that I was much more careful about washing in the river after my first experience of that!

In a Yanomami village a family would claim a section, putting their hammocks in a triangular pattern with the family fire in the middle. The fire was key as it stopped most insects from coming around at night and provided both warmth and a stove. I cautiously sat on one of the hammocks on my first visit to a village. The village leader would proudly bring gifts to us – a handful of caterpillars to eat, and the family/village gourd from the communal water store.

When I am asked about eating caterpillars I quickly explain that with this delicacy there are two types – boiled and roasted. The disadvantage of the boiled is that when you eat them they are more squishy than the roasted – a feeling that you really do *not* want to sense as you chew the twenty or so that is all part of being polite.

Sanitation and Western customs sometimes brings an interesting mix of cultures. When a Yanomami needs to blow their nose they exhale into their hand and then throw it onto the ground. To an Indian, cloth is a luxurious item. Mucus is the lowest of the low in the list of valuables! Therefore it was always with a sense of humour on the part of the Indians that we would blow our noses with its useless contents onto a valuable piece of cloth and then – horror of horrors – gently fold it and keep it in our pockets! When you think about it like that, it is a bit of a bizarre ritual. The village toilet was the ground and trees.

Since they were nomadic, a village was seldom in the same place for more than a year or two. The nomadic form of life gave some of the strongest Christian leaders an idea. They trained up and appointed various men to be itinerant evangelists. This was also somewhat problematic because there was distrust amongst the tribes.

The most common cause of death with the Yanomami used to be from war/inter-tribal fighting. The most common cause of fighting and war was the stealing of one woman from another village or tribe. I believe that the reason for this bravado was mostly intoxication.

A certain number of times in a year there was a village-wide celebration. Drugs were involved – found naturally in the wild. When a man of the tribe died, they burned his body and took his ashes, putting them in a gourd. On the anniversary of his death the ashes were mixed in their intoxicating brew.

To take the drugs, one man took a blowpipe of sorts and placed the hallucinogenic in one end. The opposite end was placed at the nostrils of another man. The first man then blew the substance through the pipe and into the nostrils of the second. The substance could be lethal. A certain amount of the same drug was placed on the arrows or darts that the skilful Indians used to shoot their game – monkeys, parrots, etc. The drug was a heavier dose than that used in celebrations and actually immobilised the animal or bird, whereupon it fell from the trees (often 100 feet tall) right to the feet of the hunter. A rock or heavy branch was used to kill the creature. Sometimes they were skinned but mostly thrown on an impromptu barbecue made of criss-crossed twigs with a fire under it. Yes, I have dined on monkey legs and parrot and other delicacies of the jungle.

Festivals were held at the New Moon, at the anniversary of someone's death or for a successful hunt. The women were kept busy beforehand chewing up the cooked manioc (cassava) root and then spitting it into a large container. This was then fermented until it turned into a very potent mixture. As the celebration continued, the men became intoxicated and high on the drugs, and made boasts of whose wife they could get. This sometimes led to a drunken raid on a village possibly three to five hours' walk away.

A Yanomami woman shaved the top of her head in a round pattern to show the scars of her being fierce. It could have come from a fight with their husband or even from a man from another village 'stealing' her. The women lived longer than the men and, after marrying at thirteen or fourteen, could be widowed three times by the age of twenty. The oldest man that I met was approximately thirty years old but looked about 100. We called him Socrates because he had that elderly, wise look about him.

One time, as the missionaries told their Bible story besides one of the fires at a village, I began to see that the mama and papa of the hammocks that we were at seemed to exhibit a twinkle in their eye, along with a slight misgiving. It was not until I went to leave after our three-hour visit that I began to see tension arise. I stood up and there was a great deal of discussion that seemed to escalate. It led to the point that my left arm was being pulled by the missionaries and my right arm by the mama and papa! A small teenage girl seemed to be caught in the middle of the argument somehow. After some time we quickly left the village and I was filled in on the potentially dangerous situation.

It seemed that when I sat down I had chosen to sit on the hammock of a young, unmarried teenage girl. In their culture that was the same thing as coming to Mama and Papa with a diamond engagement ring and asking for her hand in marriage! I was betrothed! The argument had come about because I needed to do the *honourable* thing – having made a binding contract!

One day I encountered death face-to-face, so to speak. My sister had been treating a man with some sort of a disease and he had died. His young widow stayed in our house with the dead body. It was quite bizarre to see an almost naked teenage girl in our home wearing a feather-filled ski jacket which one of the missionaries had loaned her – with her recently deceased husband lying nearby. I also contemplated about how many times she would be a widow before dying in her twenties or thirties as a result of war or disease. Sociologists had come to the area and had told the missionaries that they should not change the Indians' way of life. One of them even lived wearing just a loincloth for a number of years with them.

One could see that their current life was unsustainable. The government was always accusing the missionaries of being there to steal gold and diamonds. Nothing was further from the truth. We were there to share the unselfish love of Jesus and His plan for this remote tribe!

That night I found it very hard to sleep knowing that a corpse was in the next room and his widow grieving outside. It was just a harsh reality of this life that I had to learn.

As there were a few of us young men visiting that summer, and my sister was new to the jungle, it was decided that we would have an initiation/training programme. We learned how to make a stove out of mud and water, how to identify poisonous plants and animals and a number of very helpful things. Then afterwards a couple of Indian guides took all of the male missionaries to the middle of nowhere and we made a camp. For a week we were going to live out in the wilds of the Amazon jungle. My fear, thankfully, did not rise up – well, other than what would be normal when sleeping with wild animals and *no tent!*

It was decided that we would make camp right beside the Amazon River, near where it washed over some rocks. This would give us fresh, clean water, we were told, as any debris would be washed by the rocks. I was about to sleep on a hammock with just a mosquito net to cover me and a fire nearby and even today, I shudder at the thought. I believe that God must have put me to sleep and kept me sleeping until sunrise. When I think of what must have walked by me – jaguars and wild tapirs, snakes and tarantulas… they wouldn't care about my nervous disposition!

As we went out hunting for monkeys and birds in the 100 foot or so trees, I could not see the specks that the Indians could! They had me practise shooting a rifle, but I only managed to scare an owl out of a tree. Of course, this made the Indians laugh. I remember that we walked a great deal looking for game, but the only thing we came back with was about twenty monkeys. A barbecue-type grill was set up and the monkeys just dropped onto it with a roaring fire underneath. There was no 'gutting' of the animals or even taking off their fur. The fur burnt off and the organs just popped, I would imagine. I do not remember eating anything other than a skinny arm of a monkey and some rice which was brought along.

The Brazilian diet was rice and beans with occasional meat. The Indian diet consisted of a manioc type of bread. I remember that when the manioc was cooked the juices needed to be squeezed out of it or it would be poisonous. Eating the bread itself was a bit like eating birdseed. It was not really my cup of tea, but was edible when peanut butter was added to it and toasted.

We spent a few weeks at another mission station called Mucajai. This station had been running for some years. On Sundays the Indians joined us for services, dressed in their finest – dresses for the women and shirts and shorts for the men. I can still remember one Sunday when one of the planes landed. We always had to run along the 'airstrip' – actually just a mowed part of a field – and check that there were no rocks or branches that would harm the plane. When the plane duly arrived the women were running about holding the hem of their dresses and skirts up high so as not to dirty them, or for them not to get in the way of their running. It was a bizarre juxtaposition of seeing their almost bare bottoms and their posh Sunday frocks – but not where they were intended to be!

At Mucajai I fell in love with a food that I seldom talk about – parrot stew! The parrot is a lovely bird and was in such abundant supply that the Indians would sell many of them to us after one of their hunting days. The missionaries would have a mixture of some sort of vegetables and the most delicious parrot meat. For years every time I walked into a pet store and saw a parrot for sale, my mouth watered!

There was more trust between the Indians and the missionaries at Mucajai, and both schools for adults and children and vocational training was taking place. The real practical physical purpose of the missionaries being there was to train the Indians up in buying and selling, having profitable businesses if the 'white man' ever came in great numbers. Previously a man took his hand-carved canoe (months and months in the making, from one tree), and sell it for a T-shirt or a piece of cloth. The missionaries were busily teaching the Indians the worth of things. That had not happened yet at Surucucu and the exchange rate there was one of my T-shirts for a number of arrows, or an arrow case. A bow was the most expensive as it was their very livelihood and life.

I can remember that one of the college students there at the time naively caught on to my bartering system. Seeing me trade my white T-shirts for items, he decided that these Indians needed matching underwear briefs. As soon as we caught an Indian walking around in his underwear, the missionaries clamped down on what we could and could not sell!

The number one most valuable item on the mission stations were news magazines and classic books – and Pepsi and Coke, of course! I can remember that in those ten weeks I read through all of Charles Dickens' books and a few other authors.

In spite of my paying 'lodging', food and rent, I was also expected to help build one of the missionary families' homes. Building is definitely not my forte, although I have helped to redo a number of church buildings through the years. Working in Amazon jungle heat with archaic tools and the most basic of materials was exasperating for me. I would rather have been reading through the classics.

The station itself was closed a number of years later and I do not know whether or not the missionary family's new home was ever completed. The last straw in the growing discontentment of this new location was when one of the missionary's lives was threatened. (By putting an arrow, in bow, up to someone's head, you were threatening their life.) My sister's mission decided that it was not worth jeopardising the lives of the twenty or so that lived and worked there. Sadly, within a decade most of the people in the area had been relocated or killed – due to the expansion of the Trans-Amazonian Highway and, what the missionaries had been accused of being – gold and silver miners.

One of the most monumental achievements of modern man happened while I was living with the Yanomami Indians in those jungles. In 2015 I had an on-air discussion with Sandi Toksvig, the host of a TV show that I was on. I said, 'Sandi, in July of 1969 you were seated at Mission Control Houston next to the secretary of astronaut Neil Armstrong as you watched those first men walk on the moon [her father was a journalist]. I, on the other hand, at that moment, was in the Brazilian jungle with the Yanomami Indians, listening to the moon landing on the BBC World Service shortwave radio.' It was an amazing moment and a fascinating interaction and connection of two lives in two different part of the world. That was one of history's connecting moments!

I can remember speaking in my faltering list of fifty words pointing to the moon and telling the Indians that 'tonight men are walking on that moon'. With the incredulous look (just like when one pockets their mucus) they looked at me, laughed and shook their heads using the Yanomami word for 'crazy person'! Mostly they could not understand *why*.

I was unable (then or now) to answer that question.

CHAPTER 3
The College Years
(1970-74)

You don't have to be great to start,
but you have to start to be great.
(Zig Ziglar, *Over the Top*, Thomas Nelson 1994)

My sister, Maria, had attended Barrington College in the sleepy town of upper middle-class residents just outside of Providence, Rhode Island. In her day, they still promoted the college as what they called *The Miracle Dollar Campus*. The college had been started in 1900 by a well-known Christian teacher and author, E.W. Kenyon.

It was founded originally as Bethel Bible Training School in Massachusetts. In 1923 it was relocated and renamed Dudley Bible Institute. Then in 1950 it moved again, this time to Providence, Rhode Island and called itself Providence Bible Institute. In that year they also purchased the 150-acre estate called Belton Court in Barrington in a sealed bid – won by a single dollar. It was in 1960 that it finally moved to its leafy and luxurious accommodations. Sadly, the liberal arts college could not survive on its own and merged with the more successful Gordon College, near Boston, Massachusetts in 1985.

I found the college to be just the right size and with a Christian emphasis that I enjoyed. By the time I started in September 1970, new male and female dormitories had been built and the college was very forward-looking. Some of the top Bible teachers of the day were my Bible professors, including Dr Marvin Wilson, one of the world's leading Hebrew and Old Testament authorities and a man that years later, I would both interview and befriend. Another man, an Episcopal priest, Rev Terry Fullam, brought to the college a charismatic perspective. As the priest of a thriving parish in Connecticut, in later years, he was a much sought-after speaker on the charismatic circuit and a well-known author. Another figure was Dr Roger Green, still on staff at Gordon, as is Dr Wilson. Then Dr William Buehler rounded out the Biblical Studies faculty.

I entered with a No Stated Major area of study so was passed between American Studies and America Literature. It took about three years before I began to narrow my educational aim down. At the same time everyone had to have a biblical major or minor so that was always a fall-back.

Freshman orientation was not as wild as in some colleges and universities, with debauchery and the start of a wild life quite common in those days. I began to see, however, that there was a *drinking crowd* and a *serious crowd*, both of which I did not seem to fit into. One of the first days of orientation (where 'freshies' were required to wear special beanies and do anything that an upperclassman required) was a special display of all of the activities one could be involved with. There was choir, soccer, chess clubs, the newspaper and, the one that I made a beeline to join as a DJ – the radio station. Well, maybe the words 'radio' and 'station' were misnomers. WBCW was what was called a *carrier current* radio station according to Federal FCC guidelines. What that meant is that we were less broadcast and more narrowcast. We could broadcast anywhere that a special wire was placed. We were less 50,000 watts and more sixty watts (the size of the light bulb in the studio).

This was my forte. People have always told me that my voice is a *radio voice*. It has sometimes been described as dulcet. Others have said that I was a sound-alike for Peter Jennings – a Canadian with ABC News who has since, sadly, died. Many Canadians have mistaken me for one of their countrymen. Part of the reason for that is that almost *all* of my teachers came from upstate New York, near the Canadian border. That is what I heard and that it what I spoke. Now my accent has strengthened into more Canadian with a hint of British, after more than twenty-eight years of living near London.

To many going to college or university, this is the chance to go *wild*. Parties! Late nights! No books! Wild music! That was just not my scene. I liked a combination of classical music, what was called MOR (Middle of the Road), folk music, instrumental, original sound track recordings from films and solo artists. Jazz was also mixed in there and, of course, Christian – more contemporary than 'gospel'. I developed a particular sound (successful, I was later told, with the girls) that caused my radio programme to be turned on in public buildings at the college while other DJs were wild and loud and immediately shut off.

I became what was called the musical director of the station very quickly, and my friend, D, was the station manager. I was actually in line for his job, but took a semester away in studies in England. D, from Nutley, New Jersey, became one of my best friends and forty-five years later we still correspond and have met up once in London. We even started our own window cleaning business in college. One of our customers also hired me for babysitting jobs and I remember putting the nappy on the wrong way on his baby. But the Angell family (the father's name was also David) were very patient with me. For some years this job continued and I was to know the insurance agent and his wife and family quite well. Some years later I learned that David started writing for a TV show called *Cheers* and then for *Wings* and then *Frasier*. Sadly he and his wife died when their plane was crashed into one of the Twin Towers in New York City on that fateful day on 11 September 2001. Quite oddly I also knew a victim on board another of the planes. I had interviewed, for radio, famous actor Anthony Perkins (known for his role in the original film Psycho) and met his wife, Berry Berenson, and their child. Sadly, Berry also died in one of the planes on that day.

One day that I will always remember I learned in the newspaper that nearby Newport, Rhode Island, was to host the filming of a $6.5 million Paramount Pictures adaptation of F. Scott Fitzgerald's *The Great Gatsby*. Starring Mia Farrow and Robert Redford, it was the biggest and most expensive film ever made. Filming at the beautiful Rosecliff house and estate, it was almost too much for a TV and film fan (though having watched only a few movies in a cinema due to the restrictions of my church) like me.

I began telephoning the hotel I had been directed to as the production site and location of the PR/publicity manager Bruce Bahrenberg (I later discovered he was a close friend of Robert Redford). In my late teen voice I told Bruce that I was interested in being on set for a radio programme that I would be producing for a local radio station. 'Sorry son. It's a closed set and no one is allowed on it.' Knowing the area well, I began phoning all of the major hotels in Newport asking for Robert Redford, Mia Farrow, the film's director, Jack Clayton, and anyone I could think of that was connected with the production. After a dozen or so fruitless phone calls I finally rang what I thought was another hotel and was met with, 'Hang on. I will put you through to the room of someone who can help you.'

'Hi. I am David Sullivan from WBCW and I am interested in…' I gave my spiel but was interrupted.

'David,' the man said, 'do you know who this is?'

Stumbling with my words, I said, 'Umm. No?'

'This is Bruce. We have already spoken.'

'Ummm…' was all I could get out.

'I'll tell you what, son. Because of your persistence I *am* going to let you on set. Come on…'

I could not believe my ears. I was going to be allowed on the set of the biggest film ever produced along with *Woman's Wear Daily* and a few other 'exceptions.' Bruce later wrote a book all about the filming – but I am not included anywhere in it.

From time to time I would read the satirical *Mad* magazine with the mythical 'Alfred E. Neuman'. Sometimes they would include, in the magazine, some joke stickers which looked very authentic. I happened to find in one issue, a yellow sticker with black letters – exactly like professionals in the media use. It said, in large letters, 'PRESS'. However on top of that word it said 'If you' and underneath 'on this windshield it will get dirty'. The humorous sticker was made to be put on a windscreen and be a joke. I took the sticker, cut out the funny parts and mounted it on cardboard. For years this was what I used for my 'official' Press Pass – a sticker from *Mad* magazine. I guess you could say that another of my traits, besides persistence, is being resourceful.

Driving onto the set of *The Great Gatsby* was a wonderful experience. In my imagination I thought about, one day, actually working on film sets and having real passes and being able to spend all day learning about filming and being on set. I thought about the delicious and extravagant meals that were laid on for the cast and crew.

I had brought a cassette recorder, a bit large for those days – about twelve inches long by about eight inches wide. I hid it inside a plastic briefcase with the microphone wire coming out of it into the palm of my hand. It had an 'On' and 'Off' switch handily right on the mic so I would not run the batteries down.

So there I stood – in a sort of line with four other people – one with a camera from Channel 5 in Boston, and a few others. The ballroom scene was amazing, the costumes a wonder to behold in their 1920s jitterbug style, designed by one of the top movie costume designers of the day. The music was canned. I can remember that the song 'Kitten on the Keys' was the one in this particular scene. Then, without warning, coming right up to us was Robert Redford, along with his son in a cowboy outfit with fringes, and another child. He walked right up to the first person in the line, stared them in the eyes and barked, 'You – OUT!' Then to the second 'You – OUT!' then the third. He then glared at me and moved on. I was the only one left standing!

Mia Farrow, if I remember correctly from the newspapers, had a stand-in for the dancing scenes. The former TV *Peyton Place* actress turned girlfriend of Frank Sinatra (she vacationed with him on his yacht in nearby Tiverton, Rhode Island) was actually pregnant with her fourth child at the time but kept it under wraps in more ways than one.

After watching the production for a few hours I went back to college elated, and turned the experience into a thirty-minute radio programme. I had been bitten by the radio production bug and the movie bug at the same time.

Near my home and college stands the beautiful Cape Cod. It used to be the place of dream vacations. The rich and famous (former President Obama has holidayed on one of its most famous islands – Martha's Vineyard) have always flocked there.

Throughout the little jut of land are dotted what are called Summer Playhouses where seasoned actors and actresses and 'has-beens' put on traditional musical theatre and plays. One summer I saw a fascinating production of *Fiddler on the Roof* with *Star Trek's* Leonard Nimoy – a very kind and considerate man with amazing talents.

After sending a number of letters about my upcoming series (at that point simply called Interview and often confused with Andy Warhol's magazine by the same name), one playhouse, in particular, invited me to Monday Night Opening Celebrations – for the entire summer. That lasted for four years! I was able to interview my teen heart-throb, the late actress Patty Duke Astin and her husband, John Astin (Gomez in the TV show *The Addams Family*). In front of her husband I had the chance to live my fantasy and put my arm around Patty, asking 'Are you and your husband ready for your interview?' That is still one of the favourite photos in my life. Their son Sean is now known worldwide (and a Christian I am told) from the *Lord of the Rings* film series and other appearances.

I interviewed Barbara Bel Geddes before she became the matriarch on the popular TV series *Dallas*. In my extensive radio interviewing series the list of my guests is almost as long and prestigious as, now, my TV guest list is: 'Buffalo Bob' Smith (from *Howdy Doody* fame), Ethel from *I Love Lucy* – Vivian Vance, actor David McCallum (from *The Man from U.N.C.L.E.* TV series to *NCIS*), world-famous drummer Buddy Rich (just before his untimely death) to The BeeGees (more about THAT event later) to singer Cliff Richard (a Christian) to Gilbert O'Sullivan. One week (like our inspirational TV series that we produce now) was a Christian and one week a non-Christian. Other guests have included evangelist Jack Wyrtzen, Brother Andrew (whom

I also interviewed for TV) and Rupert von Trapp (one of the von Trapp family from *The Sound of Music*). Years later I interviewed his niece Elisabeth von Trapp for one of our TV series.

The interviews really opened up a new world and, if they were musicians, I also received great tickets for the concerts of my guests. Which leads me to a story about how I became a 'geek hero'!

I had permission to interview the BeeGees before a concert they gave at a huge arena in Providence, Rhode Island. I had also had complimentary front row and centre tickets to their concert afterwards. You must understand that I was not at all a 'ladies' man', as they used to say. I had only gone on a handful of dates in my life. A girl in college who was the captain of the cheerleaders was very beautiful and seemed to have a great personality. She was the kind of girl that you looked at and said, 'No chance for a date.' Having a trump card of meeting the BeeGees and tickets for their concert front and centre seemed like a good calling card and a great advantage. I marched over to the girls' dorm, after many rehearsals of doing it, and asked at the front desk for someone to knock on her door. I knew her a little bit as her brother was a friend. I had just never spoken with her – only admired from afar. She came downstairs and I, stupidly, reminded her who I was. As I said before, many of the girls listened to my show and liked my music. A DJ back then was similar to being a rock star years later – only on a much smaller scale.

'I was wondering if you'd like to go out to dinner with me next Friday.'

'Umm, maybe,' was her reply.

My heart was jumping up and down. I had a maybe from the captain of the cheerleaders and a great girl.

'I have to do a little bit of work afterwards, if that is OK. I am going to be interviewing the BeeGees.' I undersold this dream date.

'Really?' she asked.

'Yes, and oh, I have also a couple of tickets for us to watch the concert – front row and centre.'

'Yes, that would be great,' was her reply.

Within twenty-four hours I had all sorts of geeks and what the world would call 'no-hopers' telling me '*You* have a date with *her*? I now have confidence to ask so and so out for a date. Thank you for being such a hero!' It was funny, it was heart-warming and it helped so many other young guys grappling with their own spots and insecurity.

The date went well and we got on great but, for some reason, I never followed it up. I must have just sensed that that direction was not God's will.

It was quickly coming up to 1973. My sister and I had hatched a plan to revisit England again together, only on a longer basis. She was preparing to study Tropical Diseases at St Pancras Hospital in London that year. I made plans to attend a college in England at the same time. It had never been done at my college before – an exchange course of this kind. It took reams of letters and paperwork and sorting out with the British education system. A hiccup in the works was that my sister decided to take the course in Toronto, Canada instead, but I was still eager to attend a British university/college. As I was now tending towards studying education, I decided to apply to a college of education (which became Kingston University). My professors in the US were excited because the British education system became the thing to study as they were attempting things such as 'the open classroom', A.S. Neil's Summerhill experimental school (which I recently visited and interviewed his daughter who now runs the school), Montessori schools and other innovative programmes. I received the long-awaited letter (an aerogramme back in those days) inviting me to take the courses – just three weeks before they started in January 1973! The timing was great as I had just gotten over a short, failed romance with another girl – this one from Long Island, New York – and was utterly devastated (yes, I was at *that* age).

I jumped in with both feet into my course of educational studies. I met three young ladies. They were the first ever 'charismatics' I had ever spent time with and they would teach me praise and worship songs after classes once a week. They also helped me share the taped interview and testimony of Cliff Richard with my class. I understood from them that there were many Christians at this particular college of education because *all* of the RE department staff were committed Christians. Religious Education has been a required subject in British schools for many, many years. One of my tutors wrote a large number of Christian books that were widely read. I enjoyed the fellowship of the girls and tried asking then out on dates, but they always seemed 'busy'.

We went to Shakespearean plays in London as part of our courses, travelled to other colleges and universities and I quickly joined the Christian Union which was made up of 100 per cent charismatics (because the non-charismatics left in anger that there were so many 'happy clappies'.)

The time flew by quickly and I tried to use every moment. Petula Clark was a great favourite of mine and so I put her on my list of interview guests for my growing radio show. Although based in Switzerland with her family and husband, Claude, she was staying at a hotel in London while filming a musical ITV series. Every day I would phone the hotel and talk to Claude. 'She can't make it today,' he would say. 'Try again tomorrow.' Finally I called and Claude (I thought), a bit hoarser than usual, answered.

'Hello?' I said. 'Claude?'

'*No!* This is Petula!' a female voice squeaked through.

There in the red phone box my face was redder than the paint on it. She was sweet and considerate. She told me that that day she was filming the last TV programme, but gave me her sister's London telephone number (since lost) and her personal telephone number in Switzerland and address (since lost). I mentioned that I was planning on going to Switzerland so she invited me to stay at her home!

My interview with Cliff Richard was actually my first ever UK radio interview. I had forgotten to replace the batteries back in the recorder and did the first part of the interview without batteries. I then, embarrassed, had to stop the interview and begin it again. It was recorded at the old Talk of the Town – at that time one of London's most famous venues. I remember Cliff arriving in a very fancy car, and wearing a fur coat. Our photo together is another of my favourites; the years and clothes have changed, but not the faces. Cliff has now celebrated over fifty-nine years in show business. I continually try to contact him to do a follow-up interview but it has not yet taken place.

Getting permission to interview Gilbert O'Sullivan at the famous MAM offices was a dream! MAM were the offices of the legendary Tom Jones and Engelbert Humperdinck (in 1973 they were both just as famous). I still remember Gilbert and I having a cup of tea together before the interview and he, nosing about the day's post, finding a gold record for Tom Jones. He opened it, dreaming of the day that he also would have one. We were supposed to have a follow-up TV interview in 2015 but that also has not yet happened.

My last year at my college in the States was busy trying to get all the work accomplished that I needed to – especially after having taken half a year off for my British studies – which I received full credit for. After the experiment of my own exchange programme, the college took on board others' ideas like this, and that became one of the most popular parts of studying at Barrington College. My most unpleasant memory was one education course that I had to take at the college. On this course we studied the concept that exams were counterproductive. Half tongue-in-cheek I stated to some of the class members that since that was the case, we should not have to take any exams in that subject. Everyone said that they stood behind me. I stood up in class announcing that the class, as a whole, felt that if this was a genuine belief then we should not take any exams in that particular course.

'Who also stands up with David and believes that?' demanded the professor.

Not one single person sided with me and I learned the loneliness of standing up for something you believe in and the false support that others sometimes give.

The final course that I needed to pass was called Creative Arts – teaching children to be as creative as they can be. The bulk of the course grades were dependent on one project – building a city of the future. The dimensions were given and what should be used – paints, materials, etc. I took the road less travelled – and paid the price.

My theory on the project was that in the 1980s, 1990s and the next millennia the world would be awash with rubbish and trash. Many things would be recycled (a newish concept in 1973). Therefore my entire project would be made of recycled materials – straws, paints, soda cans, etc. And it would be round (when the required dimensions suggested that everything be square or rectangular). I made round buildings, with straws as connecting tubeways between the towers. This is now one of the most accepted designs in use today! Recycled paint covered the soda cans cum office and living blocks. It was covered over by a dome to keep climate controlled, with rain being recycled. It was basically a round Heathrow Airport Terminal 5!

I failed the course. The professor had allowed students to grade each other. Since all of their projects looked exactly the same, used the same stick figures and poster paints, block square houses and offices, mine was deemed unacceptable by the students. After receiving my grade, I appealed to have it changed, but the professor said that since my peers had given me the grade, it could not be changed.

I, to this day, sometimes tell people that I am so creative that I failed Creative Arts for being too creative! Because of that I had to take a summer course after my conditional graduation. Thus I worked a night-shift job that summer as a security guard, had one hour's sleep and then attended a children's music workshop to get the needed point grades to receive my diploma officially.

CHAPTER 4
Entering the Ministry
(1974–89)

This Book will keep you from sin
or sin will keep you from this Book.
(from a quote by D.L. Moody)
(This was written by my parents in my very first Bible that they
gave to me.)

After graduation from college and teaching in a Christian school for part of a year (where the financial remuneration was not quite what was promised, as the church that sponsored it decided to build a new church building instead), and a short stint speaking at churches across England, I ended up back at my alma mater – Barrington College. I was appointed as the financial services assistant. My boss was the treasurer of the college, and anything that had to do with finances went across my desk. It was an immense job and I learned most of it on the trot, so to speak. The daily intake from the college book store, the oversight of my cashiers, the student loans, grants – everything had to be accounted for and checked and double-checked and reported on. It was not really my thing, but I was able to take some courses for free in my areas of interest. First I audited a course in biblical Greek, which was fascinating. Then I took a media course to top up my qualification on the subject. Media had not been offered when I was studying there full-time so I found this exciting. It also allowed me interaction with the students, which I always loved and even miss now. Pouring into young people's live is such a joy to me.

From time to time I had crank callers and obnoxious parents. In nine times out of ten I let their banter roll off me. But one day a parent called who could not understand the figures, no matter how I explained it to them. They seemed quite intelligent, but were stuck in their mode of interpretation of these figures. After a thirty-minute phone conversation of swings and roundabouts, the parent said to me, 'I can see that this conversation has been a waste of time.' To which I replied, 'Well, sir, the feeling is mutual.' Little did I know that this was the college president's golfing buddy and I was demoted within a few days. My position was taken by the treasurer's new son-in-law. My new role as accounts payable supervisor was a contactless, dead-end job (at least for me) with no prospects, interest or life anywhere in it. It was pushing papers from nine to five!

About this time I has started sensing God's leading me into full-time pastoring. I applied to one or two pastorates and then found an opening with a tiny country church in rural Vermont. There were about 500 residents in that little town – one Protestant church and one Roman Catholic church. Most of the men and all of the deacons were cattle farmers, I think eventually supplying milk to Ben & Jerry's ice cream. There was also a gas station owner. I preached my first trial sermon to them and a vote of the twenty or so congregation was taken. I was their new pastor!

Full of ideas, full of plans, the church started growing and we had up to 100 members. I wrote Christmas and Easter musicals myself, featuring every person in the church that volunteered, and had special youth programmes. Our church had 20 per cent of the town's population. Some of the older deacons who were up at 3am to milk cows fell asleep during the sermons, but I felt that the church was going somewhere.

I had taken on the role with part-time pay and a parsonage. Not quite a vicarage, but I was grateful! It was actually an old trailer that one of the members had graciously donated rent-free for a year. When the first heavy storm of historical proportions hit, I learned that the pipes underneath would freeze in the -30 Fahrenheit cold until spring. A 50lb bag of potatoes that had been donated to me turned into what sounded like a bag of giant marbles as they froze stone cold in the *inside* porch of the trailer.

My enthusiasm to reach the area seemed to know no bounds. Whatever the church did *not* want to venture into, then a charity that I had help to found could help out. Through that work we started a Christian bookshop in a nearby town that also helped to double the church size. With counselling services, Christian books, Bibles and Sunday school materials, it gave people access to things that the small town would never otherwise have been able to supply.

My salary went from part-time, with me working as a cashier in a grocery store, to full-time. The youth group was bursting at the seams. We took people on trips, special events, and on Sunday evenings visited other churches to encourage them. What an exciting time!

I was able to change the leadership of the church so that every leader was a born-again committed Christian. I started groups at the church on learning about the Holy Spirit and attended the FGMFI (Full Gospel Businessmen's Fellowship International). It was while at one of the meetings that, as one leader put it, 'I ventured too close to the Jordan River' and suddenly I was on the other side. I had received what was called the Baptism with the

Holy Spirit! The Bible that I had heard for decades suddenly took on new meaning. I understood it as *'the Word of God'* – not just a Bible. The Holy Spirit spoke to me, directed me and guided me.

One day in the midst of this 'fervour' and 'anointing', I received a call from a new woman in church, one I had led to the Lord.

'It's my husband. I'm at the hospital and the doctor has told me to prepare for his funeral. He is not expected to make it through the night,' she said.

'I'll be right there and pray for him,' I offered. I went into the hospital and felt this dark and evil force trying to push me out of the Intensive Care Unit (ICU). I had always hated visiting hospitals. I started to turn back, but then recognised it for what it was.

I found the room and saw the face of a man in his last moments. He looked over to me and I said, 'I am your wife's pastor. Jesus died so that you can live. You need to repent and turn your life over to Him – if you have just a few minutes or years. He wants to be your Saviour and Lord. Can I pray with you to receive Jesus?'

My appeal was simple and straightforward. He looked at me and nodded his head 'yes' and I prayed for him. After the prayer I said to him, 'You know Jesus did not just die for your sin, but He died for your healing. Would you like me to pray for your healing?' He nodded in the affirmative again. I then used every scripture I could think of with God's healing promises *for the now* – since we will *not* need healing in heaven. I left the room.

The next morning I called the ICU and asked what condition the man was in. They took an unusually long amount of time and I expected the worst. Finally a nurse came to the phone.

'I'm sorry that I took so long, but for the first time since he's been here, he wanted to sit up and look out the window, so we had to take his tubes out.'

Both that man and his wife became regular attenders at our church. Every place they went they both shared their exciting testimony of God's saving and healing grace. Many years later he went home to be with the Lord, but his wife never stopped to thank me for bringing life into that home – and God for the extra years.

Being a Spirit-filled Baptist in America is not like it is in Britain. The two are, in most churches, incompatible. In spite of this, the leaders decided to cut back my salary to part-time so that they could invest in a new boiler! For years I had been praying that God would either turn the church on fire with the Holy Spirit or make it into a restaurant. Now we had members choosing a furnace over ministry. I sadly resigned and said that they had made their choice. Ironically, some years later someone sent me a newspaper clipping about the fire that had burned down the church building that the people had begun to worship instead of God, so I believed. Cause of fire, according to the Fire Department? The new furnace that had been installed.

From there I started doing evangelistic ministry – renting hotel and conference rooms, putting up posters and praying for people – by the ones and twos. People were staying away in droves. I can remember an instance where I set everything up in a hall – sound, music, and so on, and no one came. I sensed God tell me to 'just preach the message anyway', and I did. Later I returned the key to the janitor and he said, 'I heard that there were not too many people there.' It was then that I realised that I had been sent to be faithful so that one man could hear the gospel message.

I finally ended up back in the area of the New England where I had grown up, and started attending a new church plant. I went to the Sunday meetings and the midweek home Bible study at the co-pastors' home (husband and wife were both pastors). This was near Newport, Rhode Island, and near the huge US Navy base that used to be there. One of the Navy men took the Wednesday Bible study, alternating it with the wife co-pastor.

One week she asked me to do a 'guest slot' and God blessed it so mightily. I then began alternating with the Navy man. People would ask for cassettes of my teaching, so I would record them and come with first a few then a whole box of tapes that people were taking like sweets and giving a donation to our charity in return. They were then making copies and sharing them with their friends and families. The man from the Navy finally bowed out of teaching because he said that he realised that there was such an anointing on my teaching.

One family who were so blessed by my teaching of God's Word that they asked me to come and teach at a one-off event at their home just near Cape Cod. I drove the one hour (at that time) and taught like I'd never taught before. The one-off turned into a weekly event lasting, sometimes, until one in the morning. I was able to get into depths of God's Word that I had ever seen before. For years the name of that town, Mattapoisett, became synonymous in our ministry with my teaching of the depths of God's Word and the dedication to grow in the Lord. God blessed the business and jobs of the people whose house we met in. We were averaging twenty plus people with finances coming in for the work to flourish.

About this time I started visiting another church and then was asked to be the associate pastor of that large church. It averaged about 500 people and the leader was a seasoned Assemblies of God pastor from Texas. His sister was a well-known healing evangelist with close connections with pioneering faith healer (as the press called him) Oral Roberts and his family.

Again people came to hear when I taught the depths, but I learned something different – that the teaching of the depths of God's Word are *not* followed by the masses. The pastor would teach on simple, basic things – faith, prosperity, *me theology* – and people loved that level. When I would teach, there was a dedicated core of people but the more me-orientated Christians did *not* like to be challenged to grow. They were happy with where they were. One family in particular, the Tambaschis, really grew by leaps and bounds and to this day lead one of the churches that I helped to plant. They have been such a blessing to me and God's ministry.

After a couple of years, the senior pastor met me privately. I had been having a semi-official Bible study at home where our group was looking to, one day, plant a church. It was under the wing of this church but also ready to fly. 'I think you're ready to launch,' said the pastor. He had at first offered riches unimaginable to stay faithful to him and toe the line of every good and bad and odd teacher and evangelist who came in to the church. I could not do that. One week a man came in to the church and stated that, at one point in my teaching, 'the Holy Spirit will come' (I had thought that happened 2,000 year before). 'When that happens everyone must be on this side of the church or you will *not get the Holy Spirit.*' Sure enough in the midst of a sentence he yelled out, 'He's here. He's here. No, sister, not *there*. The Holy Spirit is only *here* (pointing to an imaginary line).'

People would ask me, 'From the biblical standpoint, is this real?' I would have to show them why something was not biblical. That was treasonous in that church, and made it more and more uncomfortable to minister there.

The pastor's sister had a large TV ministry and she would come into the area for TV productions. I would quite often drive her to the TV station and to her meetings. One time I had a whole van full of some of the top American faith preachers – household names in some circles. I had dreamt about the great nuggets I would hear and become a spiritual giant applying them. Instead I heard:

'Do you have that new Rolex with all those diamonds?'

'Yeah. My wife and I both have one.'

'How about that new Mercedes? Do you have one of them?'

'Yup. We both have one. Pastor X in Germany really helped fix me up with a good one.'

Ugh! This was one side of Christianity that I hated and detested – and yet had to see again some years later.

I was asked to preach at a new church plant from the large church that I was associate pastor of in a nearby city one Sunday evening. After I preached at the service, I asked a young man with me, a youth from our church plant, 'Do you feel like eating something?'

'Maybe. What about you? What would you like?' he questioned back.

My reply was, 'I have this feeling for pepperoni pizza.' I then looked up. 'Oh, look. There's a pizza place right here. Let's go in.' We went in and met the owner, Arthur. 'What are you doing in these parts tonight?' he asked.

'Oh, I was just preaching at a church nearby.'

'That's fantastic,' was Arthur's reply.

'Why is that?' I quizzed.

'Because I am a Christian too. I work here every day – even Sundays. This morning I prayed and asked God to bring in some Christians so that I could get some building up. And there you are.'

We rejoiced in that and I have told that story of how God can use a hankering for pepperoni pizza to guide a person.

Some months later I told the woman evangelist about this story and she said, 'We're right in the area. Let's stop by and see Arthur.' So there we came – a famous TV evangelist and entourage and me to bless this young man in his walk with the Lord. She gave him some of her tapes and books and he was blessed to know that I had remembered him.

For some months I had driven around the city where the Bible study was based and had felt led to one street and then a particular building that was an abandoned church. For those two years I felt that God had led us as a group that that building was for us. But the people who owned it did not want to sell. One Wednesday evening the phone rang. We had begun putting together a deposit for the church building that we believed 'was ours'.

The man on the phone said, 'We're ready to sell the church and not rent it. Are you ready to buy?'

'Yes!' was my excited answer.

With the signatory (someone who promised to pay if we reneged on our payments) being the husband of the home in Mattapoisett where we had such powerful services, we bought the building. Within seventeen months the building was paid off. The bank that we borrowed the money from was so impressed that they said, 'Whenever you need money for a new building or land, just let us know. We'll get it for you.' Wow! What a powerful testimony.

Sadly as a church group we moved into the new building with almost none of the regulars who had been praying and believing for the building. But God still filled it!

One Wednesday night I was teaching God's Word. We had a Sunday morning, Sunday evening and midweek meeting. I felt, strongly, God telling me to invite the people back to church on

Thursday for an unscheduled miracle meeting. We had maybe twenty people that night. Our building fund, to pay off the church, stood at about 80 per cent and we needed about $5,000 to pay it all off. The next night came and the church was full – about 100 people for this miracle service. Many new people were attending church for the very first time.

I preached a powerful message and some became new believers that night – some becoming lifelong members of one of our church plants. A few people received spectacular healings in their body. Afterwards, a man I had never met said, 'I want to pay off the balance on your building. Whatever it is.' I had made a miracle service for *others* to receive and here *I had received* a miracle! People still talk about how amazing that one service was. After a few years, we turned the church over to new leadership and planted another church in a nearby state, which is still growing to this day.

Around this time and through these years, a TV ministry was born and grew called PTL (or the legal name, Heritage Village Missionary Church). Its leaders, Jim and Tammy Bakker, I knew in a 'second-handed' way – I knew some of their leaders and we worked with their counselling department and had people referred to our church when they phoned for help. I would visit their facilities, Heritage Village, TV studios and offices and then, years later, their larger Heritage USA facility. People would say that it was like 'having a little bit of heaven on earth'. People would sing, pray, teach, preach all across the property. There were different activities going on for every age group. It was the most well-organised and executed place that I think I have seen in my life. Theology aside, it was uniting the Body of Christ. On one of my visits there I had an unfortunate thing happen and a devastating theft took place. Without knowing me, over $1,000 in various items, repair work and extras was donated to me. I believe that they were sincerely trying to follow Jesus, but were waylaid in their plans with a number of unscrupulous other evangelists and pastors with evil in their hearts.

I even explored the idea of planting a church near that location in South Carolina. The weather and beauty of nature was overwhelming. As I travelled there in the springtime I heard what I felt was the voice of the Lord saying, 'What if that man (Jim Bakker) was no longer there?' What would happen to this whole area?' I then realised that *any* ministry centred on a *man* is liable to failure. Billy Graham discovered this and, his whole life, prepared for passing on his 'baton' of ministry. I knew that this 'testing of the waters' was an exploratory venture to see what God wanted, and He did not want this. Within a few years of that trip, a moral failure was discovered and the US government, using a law intended for the Mafia's use of the telephone lines, tried to put Jim away for life – for offering too many overnight stays in exchange for a certain level of donations towards the construction of more rooms.

Later, as a church, we bought 120 acres of land to build a PTL-style church and retreat centre. At one point I had to take over the payments myself, because many of the people just wanted the security of the little church building without enlarging the place of our tent. I had felt led that if there were any problems, we should sell sooner rather than later. After a real estate agent tried to sell the beautiful land, without success, I decided to try to sell it myself. I had over 100 contacts of interest and sold it within months for many times the original sale price.

For years I began to go to England to speak at churches and Bible institutes, and to attend the newly established Christian Resources Exhibition. I was at the very first one and got to know the owners of it very well, Gos and Diana Home. Every year I would go to England for a week or two or three, and the work in England seemed to grow and the interest grew greater.

Finally I felt the call of the Lord to, once again, turn a church over to new leadership and make the step of faith to help plant churches in England.

CHAPTER 5
World Missions
(1989–97)

Ask of me, and I shall give thee the heathen for thine
inheritance, and the uttermost parts of the earth for thy
possession.
(Psalm 2:8, KJV)
(This has been my prayer for as long as I can remember.)

After having planted a number of churches and assisted with
others for almost twelve years, I had always had England on my
heart to reach – and into Europe. I had started preaching there,
usually in February of every year – the coldest month of the year
– anywhere! I sometimes spoke at Bible schools and attended or
exhibited at the Christian Resources Exhibition. It had started
as a week and a half and gradually extended until I made it
permanent! I can still remember the joy of having the visa that
allowed me to do full-time ministry in a land and with a people
that I had grown to love and pray for. In spite of Britain being the
nation from which people such as Hudson Taylor was sent out,
it had suddenly become a mostly godless nation where the same
continents that had received missionaries were now sending
them to Britain – to evangelise!

I arrived in 1989 and joyfully started the work. Within five
weeks my mother telephoned to tell me that my father had

gone home to be with the Lord. What a shock! My thoughts and emotions were up and down – joyful that he was with the Lord and Saviour that he loved, but sad that my mother had lost her lifelong companion who did everything for her – including driving her wherever she needed to go. When I was young, I used to lie in bed at night listening to them chat and sometimes joke and was so pleased that they were able to celebrate so many years together. All of the relatives had put on a fiftieth anniversary party, which was celebrated just before I left and just about six weeks before his passing.

My mother had always reminded our family that the physical body was just like an eggshell. When we die, our spirit and soul, according to the Bible, go to be with the Lord. Thus, it is like paying attention to an old eggshell when we die. I had asked my mother if she wanted me to attend the funeral, and move back, but her reply was an emphatic 'No! He would not have wanted that.' So I grieved and tried to comfort others who needed comfort in various situations. My mother eventually spent a few months with me and then a few months with my sister, Maria, then a missionary in Spain. After years of doing that, she finally decided to stay home. There were eight years difference between my parents, and when she finally went home to be with the Lord it was almost to the day, eight years later!

I had been in correspondence with a fairly new church plant that had the same vision to plant another church. A number of leaders had come and gone in a short period of time – which should have been a warning sign. I started as a volunteer. I set up a 'teens and twenties' group in the church and worked with children and youth. During the summer I was able to lead a vacation Bible school-style of summer holiday kids' club, where about 100 attended. It was based on an American Western theme which I found kids tended to enjoy. About twenty young people gave their lives to Jesus Christ during that time – a real encouragement. I was also able to start up an all-day full-time Monday Bible institute and a part-time evening one. Putting together my notes from years of pastoring in the key subjects of Christianity – including Beginning Greek – the students, young and old alike, enjoyed digging into the depth and breadth of God's Word. I preached and manned the office, where another key leader was forced out because of his stand with Israel and the Jewish people. I could hear the clock ticking. The pastor, getting on in years, spent less and less time in the office, preferring to stay and home and not be involved with answering phone calls and requests for counselling.

Finally, one day I was asked to visit one of the members. There in the house were about twenty of the church members. I was told that in my two years I had done absolutely *nothing* for the church! I am sure that everyone there knew it to be a lie. I was told that the church plant that I was to be in charge of was to be actually started by a man and his wife who, I knew, were there for just a matter of months as they were on their way to Germany! None of this was making sense to me.

The final nail was that I was told that their legal sponsorship (never financially) of me to be in the country was rescinded, effective immediately, and that I should pack my bags and go back to America! I was a 'man without a country'. I was dumbfounded – first by my legal standing and second that the people that I had done so much for and with – I had brought in so many to the Lord and had led the church when the leader just wanted to retire – were giving me a *Judas kiss* and throwing me out of the door.

Thankfully, a few families who had seen the injustice of this and who were loosely connected with the church asked me to start a church plant and would give me legal sponsorship for my visa! What a relief from Almighty God! A pastor friend of mine had a church plant also, some miles away. He was in the Armed Forces and was to leave the church and return to America. He said that it might be a good idea to merge the two church plants into one. He did caution me, though, that there were a couple of older women who liked to 'run things', as he said.

Things went well! The group began to grow. A disused Brethren chapel was vacant and I received permission to use the small building, in a quaint English village, for the church plant. I visited everyone in the village and we put on a wonderful Christmas programme. There was always this feeling, though, of what we now call a *shadow government*, so to speak! Even the owners of the building knew the reputation of the two ladies and said that the building was under my auspices and not theirs!

The son of one of the ladies was a good woodworker and I gave him the task of designing a sign for the front that would finally give us an identity in the village. I knew almost every single family there, having visited with them and having left them various invites for special events. We had called it 'X (the name of the village) Chapel' – a non-denominational church – or interdenominational church, as some would call it.

I can clearly remember showing up on a Monday morning to inspect the young man's work. I had given him the design of a smallish unassuming sign with simply 'X Chapel' on it and a contact telephone number. Instead, what I found was a massive sign with beams pounded into the ground, announcing to the world that this was 'The X Brethren Chapel'! Firstly, we had no rights to be called a Brethren church. The two women had, years ago, been associated with the group that traditionally and ironically, do not allow women to have the same voice as men.

They are to be submitted to them! So we were acting illegally in putting up a sign proclaiming something that was not true. Secondly, the son had the plans I'd given him for what to write. He sheepishly admitted later that his mother had told him not to write what I had asked. He was in his late twenties, I believe!

I called a church meeting and promptly announced that we needed to decide who and what we were. If we were a church that catered to gossip and underhanded leadership, then I would promptly submit my resignation and they would be left leaderless and without financial support. If we were a church that, as I had done, put all decisions before all of the members of the church for consultation, then I would continue as pastor.

Sadly, the church members decided that they were not able to go against these two strong-minded women. I tended my resignation and felt, once again, betrayed. Having two such events in as many years, I felt totally inadequate and returned to the States for six months, where I fully intended to forget about this very bad idea and move on. Sadly I revisited the church some years after and, like so many others, it has been turned into a private home – with no Christian witness for miles around!

For those months in America the people and land of England, Britain and even Europe tugged at my heart strings and I knew that God wanted me to continue the work that I was doing – but possibly in a new place, and with a new way of ministry!

A pastor friend of mine for a number of years lived in Hertfordshire, one of the Home Counties. I had stayed at his home one time as it was closer to London than where I was living at the time. In fact, it was just a short thirty-minute train ride to get to many things in London. He sponsored me, legally, to return to the UK and work with his London church. In fact, he and his family moved to a larger flat and I moved into his.

Everything seemed to be working out with this fresh start.

Just a few months later he told me that a woman in his church worked for an American evangelist I had slightly heard of. They were looking for someone to take over what was called 'Ministerial Relations' – a sort of public relations but with churches and ministers. In 1991 they had held a large meeting at one of London's larger venues. Now they were planning one more, at the largest venue in London, which could hold up to 15,000 people!

I went for the interview with the director, a fellow American. We got on quite well and we had a similar sense of humour. Although the pay was small, it looked like a good opportunity. It was also a regular salary, something which I had not had in many years.

From the first days I could tell that it was going to be a wild ride. There were times when the director and I could not keep a straight face when we were out together. In the office, however, it was all work and seriousness. I came up with quite a few ideas and enlarged smaller ideas that were thrown at me. Since there were two parts to the event, a closed – by registration – one and a public open event, there were people coming for the morning sessions and staying for the evening sessions. The idea that I pitched was to put together a Christian exhibition. So many ministries and churches were involved in the event that they would love an opportunity to tell who they were. Since my friends owned and ran the actual Christian Resources Exhibition I stated that I would not put it together unless I received their 'blessing'. We met with Gos and Diana Home and they not only gave permission and blessing, but also requested that their suppliers give the same discounts for stand fitting and electrics. What a blessing! What a gracious couple.

Between the main seating area of the stands and the main entrance doors there was an area in which we could fit the exhibition perfectly. In year three (the one-off turned into an annual event in London) of my putting the Christian exhibition together, I 1) was 'headhunted' to start another exhibition by another ministry; 2) had the exhibition being called by one of the national British newspapers the *Ideal God Exhibition* – a parody of the annual London favourite, the Ideal Home Exhibition.

The American evangelist, on seeing the finances roll in for this, then began telling me that the exhibition needed to pay for the 100,000 twenty-four page full-colour magazines given out free of charge at the event. The next year he raised that bar and asked for the amount to come in to actually pay for the hire of one of Europe's major venues for the week! No bonuses and, at the end, no days off in lieu of working from 6am until 1am during the event, and having to clean up afterwards! Yet it was such a blessing – that eventually lasted for five years – to be part of something that was a blessing to so many thousands of people each year!

It was a wonder to behold once we got all of the bugs ironed out. I had selected the main high flow area of the venue as what I called 'prestige stands' for the likes of major Christian book publishers, churches, church denominations – organisations that had the cash flow and wanted the high profile and footfall. The side areas were for smaller churches and new ministries kicking off and at a much smaller rate. (One quite well-known UK personality always charts her success to the special rate I gave her company at the exhibition.)

One of the strange things about Christians, I have found, is that they all think that everyone is a Christian and trustworthy. People who were exhibiting at the stands used to leave their laptops, flat screens – even money collection boxes – and walk off for an hour or two, or overnight, thinking, 'It's a Christian event. No one will steal anything.' The venue actually had an underground area hidden away, part of the London Underground Network. After a spate of thefts, the police and security looked in this hidden area and found boxes and all sorts of items from *other* events that had taken place there and had things stolen. It was a major problem for all events held there.

Working with this major American evangelist or minister was not like working for other evangelists/ministers. Even back in the days when emails were just starting, he was very hands-on. I would have direct contact with him via fax almost every day and throughout the day.

One of the funniest things that happened to me was during the event. I would come back from London to the ministry offices to check faxes, sometimes make bank deposits, etc. On checking through the faxes at about 1am I noticed one from the company that actually wrote the appeal letters for the organisation. (Many large ministries hire them and can tell you how much money will be generated from each letter.) On my way back into London, I slipped the appeal letter under his hotel room door. That was about 3am. A few months later I read that month's appeal letter that he had been given this message by the Lord at 3am one morning. It was the letter that I had slipped under his door. I told someone, 'That is the first time that I have ever been called "the Lord"!'

Another time I was asked to be the official photographer, besides my regular work, at a smaller event in another city. I took all sorts of photos and then tried to get a shot of the evangelist's back during an offering wind up – to some, the most sacred part of the entire service. All of us on the team had a camaraderie because of so much waiting for things to happen, prepping everything and other monotonous tasks. As I attempted to take a photo from the back of the stage, the evangelist turned to me and said, 'Brother, would you please sit down and take out *your* chequebook?' The organist, a friend, wove into his hymn playing the 'da-dum da-dum' that is used in baseball games when someone makes a home run. You could hear it in the tape of the meeting! No one else ever noticed.

People used to think that I was nervous around the man, but some of my fear was a bit of an act! However, as I would do almost all of his driving, I would know that he was second-guessing everything that everyone did. My only respite was fetching things for him. On one journey I went into the petrol station for a coffee for him, and a tea. Thinking to myself that I had a few minutes not to be in the firing line, I was quite calm. In making the coffees I suddenly heard, 'David! What are you playin' at?' and spilled the coffee all over myself.

Another time, his usual room at his regular hotel in London was not ready in time. So my brief was to stall him. I drove into and through every tourist attraction in London so the director would not get in trouble and the room could be made up with the evangelist's exacting requirements. Finally, going around Piccadilly Circus and Trafalgar Square, he could see that something was not quite right. He flew into London sometimes on quite small errands so he knew the city well. I was caught out!

Another time he was staying at a budget-y hotel in London and the director, at that time, was nearing the end of his tenure (although he did come back years later). I was given the task of, on my own, taking the evangelist to a new hotel and a new room (not an easy task at all). The temperature had to be set precisely, hours before, there had to be a certain brand of water in the room, no smoking – of course – and the room booked in a fictitious name. I knew the drill. We arrived at the hotel and a heavy smoker who liked a lot of heat had been staying there. I received half a head-chopping, and the director received most of it!

As I have now travelled throughout almost every continent, from closed countries to open, large cities to small villages, I did begin to understand the necessity of, if at all possible, drinking the same high-quality brand of water when travelling. Stomach bugs and unease is the most common time-stealer of travelling professionals, and by having the exact same water at every location it helps this to calm down. Another thing, which he also practised and I have taken on board, is to fast until after you preach. There are certain spiritual benefits to it and also physical ones. I notice that there is more power in my sharing of God's Word when my body is under control and not trying to recuperate after a massive meal.

I was the person who met with all of the top leaders when they came into the UK – for ministry business or for their own pleasure. Once, after spending time with a well-known TV Bible teacher, I was 'headhunted' to run their ministry in the UK and Europe. Although quite honoured to be asked, I stayed loyal and refused the offer. In hindsight it might have been a better move to accept the offer.

The evangelist had always had a favourite restaurant in London through the years. The owner, when he walked in the door, always said, 'I have something special for you.' I was near the restaurant two years ago in London on a casting and decided to have a quick bite there – for old time's sake. While enjoying a leisurely small meal, I heard one of the waiters pick up the phone and say, 'Hello, XXX. Seven o'clock? That would be fine. You're going to the theatre afterwards? That's nice. We will have your usual table.' I made sure that I finished quickly – not because I was afraid of him but because it would have been a bit awkward, I think.

A few years ago I interviewed his son, who runs a media ministry. I did not tell him that I had worked closely with his father for five years. I did ask him some questions, knowing his mother and father very well. 'Do you think that you are more like your dad or your mom?' was one of the questions. It was so funny looking into his eyes and seeing his father's eyes. I saw the same thing when interviewing Chris Watson – the father of actress and model Emma Watson. I could see those characteristic Emma Watson eyes!

Another of the projects that I was tasked with was to write a 'Counsellors' Manual' to be used at the event and then, eventually, used all over the world at all of the missions and translated into many languages. A couple of men the evangelist respected were tasked with 'assisting' me. Practically that ended up being them writing a couple of short chapters and myself the rest. I used my ministry notes that I had put together over the decades and used in training people in my church plants. It was a hit with the 1,500 counsellors and then in Paris, Holland and worldwide. I would assume they are still using it.

During the week of the event, the evangelist would hire a professional PR company to do a higher level of the PR work. One year the PR company told me, 'You know this man better than anyone else in this country. We want *you* to be the spokesperson for the event without him or anyone else finding out about it.' (While they received the commission!)

The added stress and pressure started days before with being on BBC Five Live and a panel discussion. Outside of the venue,

Channel 4 recorded a special programme on the topic of 'Is the Bible for Real?', questioning the head of the Evangelical Alliance, top London pastors and *me*. Our PA in the office said, 'You've just been on Channel 4.'

Shh!' I said. 'No one's supposed to know!'

'No one's to know? It's watched by millions of people.'

The whole week was like that. I was running around during the event and had to stop to be on a panel radio chat show with an atheist, a Catholic priest, a Jewish rabbi and someone else talking about miracles. In the midst of this, our new director called me and asked me to bring a bottle of water for him at the front of the huge venue.

'I'm really kind of in the middle of something at the moment,' I had to say.

Every year I would room with a friend of the evangelist who also served as a member of the board of directors and his driver, during the event. I had a 7am call to a radio car parked in front of the hotel but had to be secretive.

'Are you having breakfast?' the board member asked me.

'No,' I said. 'I have to do a little something.' I then scrambled down to the radio car and had a debate with the dean of St Paul's Cathedral on 'Are Miracles Real?'. I had mistakenly thought that it was being aired live but it was not.

The board member took the evangelist to a TV interview in the afternoon on British national TV and waited in the car. He turned the radio on and there was this debate airing. When the evangelist came out, the board member said, 'I've just heard David Sullivan debating the dean of St Paul's Cathedral on whether miracles are real!'

The evangelist looked to the 'paid' PR person and said 'What's this about?' The PR guy said, 'Oh, well, Pastor X (a well-known

London pastor) could not make the debate at the last moment so we asked David to do it.' (Not true!)

'Well, how did he do?' the evangelist asked.

'Great! He did a great job!'

That board member impacted my life greatly. He was getting on in years but was as spry as a twenty-year-old. He would eat some natural nuts and seeds and was as trim as could be. His greatest strength, though, was his relationship with God.

The first time I roomed with him I was awoken with a start in the middle of the night. The man was crying and crying. I thought that he must be in pain. I asked him what was wrong. He pulled his frame off the bed, looked at me through tear-stained eyes and said, 'We need to die to self, David. We must take up our cross daily and follow Him.'

All I could say was 'I know. I know.'

After this repeated for most nights and for a number of years, his message began to sink deeper and deeper into my heart. He had seen the good and seen the bad. He had lived a long life and had seen man's compassion and man's inhumanity. Yet in all of that he sifted it down to these words: the most important things in life are to *Die to self and Take up our cross daily to follow Jesus*. That is one of the messages that has impacted my life the most.

Another time I was tasked with writing the speech for the evangelist that he gave at the University of Cambridge, and the full-page advert featured in the UK newspapers was entitled 'Here I stand!' (like Martin Luther). Part of one or two of his books I ghost wrote. And then there were 'those letters'.

Instead of miracles and healing, the evangelist was being dragged into criticism about his financial appeal letters. It became so bad that he decided to put together a 'panel of UK leaders' to vet his letters. What he did not know was that I was tasked, again without his knowledge, with rewriting and anglicising the letters (since I can speak both English and American!).

Out came the terms that caused so much controversy. I did such a great job that the panel began to say, 'He is really taking our comments on board. The letters are so much more British now!'

My time with the evangelist led to some great connections, none of which were ever used for profit but for ministering. One man I developed a long friendship with came to the event from Greece. I began writing and then visiting and ministering there. This was the embryo that actually developed into what is now our worldwide ministry.

The financial supporters are a vital part of any ministry, and even though they did not have direct access to the evangelist, they could talk to me. I was the one with open ears. In this way I met some great people and some very unusual ones.

One woman came into the office to warn the evangelist about how the enemy was using radio waves. Whenever anyone picked up the phone to answer it, she would run out of the room. Another family came and explained how they were all prophets – papa prophet, mama prophet and son prophet. They were grooming the son to be *The Next Big Thing!*

One day a young couple came into the office with an idea to start a worldwide media network. I think these people were about the third or fourth that month that had come with the same vision. Basically they wanted millions to start up the work and get the necessary documents and licences. Without them knowing it, I was sent by the evangelist to dig up everything about them so that he could make a quality decision before committing any finances. I knew more about this couple then they did – their for-profit making company, the finances of which would go into their pockets, the charity that they took over from someone else whose whole aim was to raise money to donate to their for-profit media company... I even phoned the Charity Commission about this as, with my background in advising charities, it seemed quite suspect to me. I changed some of the names and purposes so as not to steer them in the right direction. The media company, I said, was a company to sell items for the handicapped. I explained fully that a charity would be started whose whole purpose was to raise money to give to a for-profit company that would end up in my or my friends' pockets.

'That would be *illegal*, would it not?' I questioned.

'Well, in a number of instances that would be quite legal.'

I notice that the main media company is now a charity, so I am not sure how and when the changes were made!

Another time I was asked to, secretly, secure a channel on a UK TV network. The evangelist's American TV show had been taken off of one of Europe's largest TV networks and laws were passed to not allow anything about healing to ever be seen again on UK TV. I made a few phone calls, had a few meetings and, *boom!* I was at Sky TV, having a grand tour of a new venture for which they were just building sets and studios. It was called 'Digital TV' and would revolutionise TV and media – which it has. By the end of the afternoon, I had in my hand an agreement that, yes indeed, I could have a religious channel on the brand-new Sky platform. After making a Friday afternoon call to the US HQ, I was thanked and that was the last I ever heard of it. It was intended to be top secret and not to be divulged even to the evangelist's son who was in charge of media outreach in the US.

One of the facets of the work that I enjoyed was finding trends in British Christianity and churches and keeping tabs with what new works and ministries were coming into London and the UK. I would then meet with the heads of them and suss out whether or not they could be tapped to become part of the event's network of churches. By the end of my time, I had been privileged to bring the number up to 1,500 churches!

I can remember in my early days with the evangelist telling him about one of those two ministers and saying that forging relationships with these two men would be key to having a successful relationship with London churches. They did indeed become the two men that influenced more Christians and church members in London in those years than anyone else.

After working with the event for four years ('Definitely the last year,' the evangelist would say), moves were made to turn the event over to one of those two ministers who had a network, at that time, of hundreds of churches and church plants across London. His main emphasis, though, was not really in this direction of putting on one of Europe's largest conferences. I was 'handed over' to him at the start of my fifth year and worked out of a tiny office in London and a bit of space back in the evangelist's office. I had no support, no staff and in this year, instead of a director and his PA and a fully staffed office, it was me, myself and I – and a computer. Needless to say, running a major operation like the event – one of the largest events in the world at that time – singlehandedly was an impossible task.

In my last year I was warned by my doctor that I would face major burnout or worse due to overwork and stress. An event of this magnitude and workload was a major event for a team of twenty or thirty. This time I was the only salaried person on whose shoulders the whole event was resting. The director was usually spending time with the speakers or the evangelist, sitting on the stage during the event or selling videos of the meetings from the platform. The PA was usually compiling the cards of the miracles happening on stage. And then there was me. There

The winner of the School yearbook contest!

Cliff Richard – 1973

Angus Buchan, author of *Faith Like Potatoes*

Tennis champion Margaret Court

New York Times bestselling author, Joyce Meyer

Praying with Mrs Yonggi Cho

Award winning film producer, Lord David Puttnam (*Chariots of Fire*)

Former Head of the British Army, Sir Richard Dannatt

Dr Young
Hoon Lee

Anne Graham
Lotz

Francis Chan

Returning from a summer with the Yanomami Indians

Brother Andrew
(*God's Smuggler*)

Darlene Zschech

Brother Yun (*The Heavenly Man*)

Douglas Gresham – stepson of author CS Lewis and producer of the Narnia films

Used by permission of Kayleigh Ghiot

Syrian refugees near the Syrian border

Senator and boxing champion, Manny Pacquiao

Praying for Dr David Yonggi Cho

were hundreds of volunteers – security, ushers, and so on, who were, mostly, from the parts of Africa where the evangelist was seen as almost a 'god'. The venue had dozens of escalators, lifts – everything that needed security watching it – especially with hundreds of small kids left to their own devices, not to mention the thieves coming into the free event nightly!

One of the main problems with overseeing the huge event was that as soon as the evangelist would hit the door at the venue, all the security decided they had to have the task of surrounding him 'for his protection'. Escalators were left unmanned and the few volunteers we had all had to go in and listen to him speak. The management of the venue would phone me every night and tell me that the escalators would all be shut down unless there was security on them. After the event I would work sometimes until 3am – especially when, some years, they had me in the 'counting room'.

The moment the event closed, everyone abandoned the venue and it was my job to either find volunteers (who had just worked long shifts and were totally beat) or do it myself. It even sometimes meant driving a truck after picking up every bit of the rubbish and other things scattered throughout the venue!

With all of this in mind and the knowledge that this year I would have more than just exhaustion and sore feet to show for a week of continual work, when it got close to the event and I knew that I would get the brunt of it, I totally stressed out and called in sick for the event. I am told that it was the most unusual one, due to it being in *new hands* and yet the evangelist wanted to leave *his* mark on it.

Legally I could not be punished for exhaustion and burnout, so I was allowed to do all the paperwork and movements of things after such a huge event. For one week I was sent to a large storage area to count DVDs, tapes, papers and so on. Right at 5pm – quitting time – I was told that my job was completed. The reason given was that I had trained up people to know how to run the event. I was told that even if I had worked myself to exhaustion during the event, I would still have been made redundant. Five years of blood, sweat and tears, of seven-day weeks presenting the event in church on Sunday, various meetings on Saturdays, and there was an end to it all.

I cannot say I was not relieved or had not counted the cost beforehand.

CHAPTER 6
Burnout and Rebuild
(1997–2004)

Winners never quit and quitters never win.
(Vince Lombardi)

The years putting the mission together had really burned me out spiritually and physically, and had affected pretty much every area of my life. Everything that could be attacked seemed to be attacked. When I would go into churches to be edified, the pastor would always recognise me and say, 'Oh, I see David Sullivan is here, such and such an event leader. Let's have him bring greetings.' I finally just stopped attending churches until I could get the *strength* and fire back in my bones. I seemed to have many of the classic signs of burnout – having lost my job that I had been successful at for five years and had now been closely associated with.

In the midst of this I continued to receive letters and emails from leaders overseas asking me to take on meetings and help to train up leaders in their cities and countries. They knew of the work that I had done, both on a large scale and on a smaller scale.

I had been filming and then putting on leadership training events throughout the world as a gift to those countries and cities. As the London event was all about mailing lists and money, I decided to give the training events to various locations to show the agape love of God. We also committed to at least two to three years so that it was not a flash in the pan but a long-term commitment to that city and nation. We started in Athens, Greece.

Greek church-ianity is very unusual. There is the thought that 'Christianity started here so we have the corner on the market'. It took me many, many trips to Athens just to get the trust of the church and ministry leaders there. We had sown a seed so deep there in those years that about ten years ago I went back to film another documentary about the country, and all of the fragmented and distrustful organisations and churches agreed to be in it! That was never heard of!

I attended meetings with pastors, meetings with groups of pastors (there is a closed fellowship where the key leaders hear out issue and projects and thumbs-up the ones they like – a bit like in Paul's days at the Areopagus). I met with people in their homes, in restaurants, in churches – anywhere I could get them to spend time meeting me and hearing about my love for the city and nation. It was more in depth than any of our London events. We knew it would be smaller but we knew also that it would grow fruit that would last.

Finally, the first event was planned at the largest church in Athens, within minutes of Omonoia Square – Athens' Times Square, where anything can happen – and does! The template that we revised depending on each location worked well: Friday night – leadership training, Saturday morning – leadership training, Saturday afternoon – using that training, the lost were reached and invited to the Saturday evening evangelistic meeting. Then there was Sunday morning at the host church and then Sunday evening at another church – all done and sponsored as a love gift to the city and nation. The pastor would, each time, take offerings, but we turned them back to him and they were put towards a new, larger building which, years later, I was privileged to sit in.

Our first *AGAPE: Athens* had about fifty leaders attending and about thirty to fifty who accepted the Lord in the Saturday evening evangelistic meeting. The next year it grew, and we were able to see some of the converts from the first year grow in the Lord. Then the third year we could see that the building would no longer hold us or the growing church. A great evangelistic concert brought in hundreds and was translated into dozens of languages. What a joy to see the nations coming to Christ.

Then the same meetings were held for a number of years near Rome, then Sweden and France and Brazil and on until we were reaching about fifty nations! I thought God was finished with me and here I was, ending up with the ministry being multiplied like fish and bread in the hands of a child, feeding multitudes!

One day I was invited to the British Parliamentary Prayer Breakfast with guest speaker Anne Graham Lotz (whom I later interviewed and became a friend to this ministry). At the table were some pastors and leaders. They asked us, one by one, to introduce ourselves. For some reason I was first, and shared what I was doing and what our ministry was all about. A pastor, still a friend, told who he was and about his church.

I sometimes try to shy away from Americans – especially when they tend to be a bit loud and brash. The man next to me, the last to share, said, with an American accent, 'Hi!! I'm George Verwer and I run this little thing called Operation Mobilisation.' I could have sunk into the floor. I felt like that if I knew who it was I would not have even mentioned our little growing ministry.

George and I got on well and through the years he has been a good friend and close adviser. He often phones just to say that he is thinking about us and praying for us.

'I think that there's a great canal in your town – is that right?' he asked.

'Yes, there is,' I answered.

'Let's make a plan one day and we'll walk it together.'

Years later we finally got our schedules to jive together and we walked the canal – after filming an interview with him for our first leadership TV series, *Principles of Leadership*.

We quite often hear, we believe, from God. Sometimes it's like a whisper, sometimes an inner witness, and sometimes it's a strong, emphatic command – not physically or audible at all, though. On one of the occasions I felt God say, 'You've done the filmmaking. You've done the ministry. Now put the two of them together.' We thought that that made sound sense and since we were already in different countries we started filming – first with a consumer camera and then with a prosumer broadcast camera. Our very first series was called Into All the World. It is still in production and has covered the stories of Christians on almost every continent.

In the midst of this filming the series, in late 2003 we planned on going to Sweden to film a documentary film about what God was doing there. Since *Livets Ord* (Word of Life) and Ulf Ekman started the first non-denominational church there, and then Bible school, we decided to approach them. Pastor Ulf and his wife had moved to Israel for a number of years so we contacted Pastor Robert Eck who took over for him. In some unknown way, Pastor Ulf got a hold of my request to interview Pastor Eck on camera and wrote to me: 'I will be arriving that morning from Israel and preaching in the morning service. Would you like to interview me instead?' Wow! Of course. This is the man with so many fantastic stories of God's leading and protection.

Pastor Ulf and his wife, Birgitta, arrived on a flight at 3am and he spoke at the morning service. Then I interviewed him, after which he attended the birthday celebration of one of his long-standing leaders. What a day!

The intent was to ask some questions about Sweden and then drop those into our film about the country. Because this was *Pastor Ulf* I decided to read his book and ask him some delving questions. For thirty minutes I asked him things such as, 'You had a bomb go off in your church sanctuary and one in your home mailbox. Your children went to school with graffiti on the walls saying "Hang Ulf Ekman!". Pastor Ulf, how do *you* handle criticism?'

Afterwards, we looked at the completed interview, using a few of the questions in the film about Sweden. Yet as we watched the thirty-minute interview we said, 'This looks more like *Principles of Leadership!* Let's film a whole series like this.' I asked my good friend George Verwer, 'Would you like to be in this series?' He agreed. I contacted Loren Cunningham, Jackie Pullinger, Joyce Meyer, Dr Luis Palau and on and on. Today we are working on completing the third fifty-two part leadership series with some of the most well-known and loved names in Christianity all sharing their lives and principles.

At the start, putting these interviews and the *Into All the World* film series on DVD was just a great way to share what God was doing with the leaders that we are connected with worldwide. During this time a friend suggested that I should attend CEVMA – the Christian European Visual Media Association – held in different venues and countries each year. It was there that I met people that made me think, 'They are as crazy as I am – trusting the Lord, and they have a vision to reach the world that same crazy way that I have – by using visual media.'

During the first meal at the conference in Switzerland, someone asked me what I did. I told him about our DVDs that we share with leaders. An Australian gentleman leaned across the table and said, 'Sorry to be eavesdropping, but I like what you are doing and we want to air your programmes on the Australian Christian Channel.' That was the start! I never would have thought that by the end of the conference four or five different TV networks would be agreeing to air our productions. Today we are on over forty Christian TV networks around the world, broadcasting to over 800 million people just our Christian TV series.

Next followed *Principles of Praise* with leading Christian singer-songwriters from every genre including Darlene Zschech, Tim Hughes, Israel Houghton, The Newsboys and others. We even interviewed Country and Western singing star George Hamilton IV. Then we started filming for *Stars in His Crown* – interviews with Christian actors, actresses, directors, producers, etc. *Principles of Prayer* is an interview series with those involved in leading Christian intercessory prayer – like Suzette Hattingh who, for years, led Reinhard Bonnke's prayer teams and Pete Greig, prayer coordinator for Holy Trinity Brompton, Angus Buchan, author of *Faith Like Potatoes* and Dr Yonggi Cho.

After beginning production of a number of series for Christian TV, we saw that the field, as Jesus said, is the world. It was then that we began to produce a number of what we call 'inspirational' TV series, like *Principles of Business*, to air on secular TV. In each programme I interview a well-known Christian business person and then, the next week, a well-known non-Christian but inspirational business person. About half the guests in this series are from China, where we work with different sectors and also with churches, charities, NGOs and ministries.

In *Next Gen & Kin* we meet various relatives of household names – Charles Dickens' great-great-great-granddaughter, C.S. Lewis' stepson, two of Billy Graham's daughters, actress and model Emma Watson's father, singer Joss Stone's mother, Peter Buffett, son of one of the richest men in the world ,Warren Buffett, and more. Another inspirational series, *Principles of Competition*, leads us into the lives of men and women like five-times world heavyweight champion Evander Holyfield, world champion boxer Manny Pacquiao, former Manchester United and Everton goalie Tim Howard, all-time tennis champion Margaret Court and others.

God has enabled me and us to develop relationships with many of these – both Christians and non-Christians. We feel that it is almost the purpose rather than the by-product of the interviews. It also helps people to delve into the things that matter in people's lives. One of the questions which I often ask my non-Christian guests is, 'What philosophical touchstone, religious belief or something someone said to you in your youth really set your course for life so that even in the difficult times you can weather the storm?' A great number of our guests tell us about their mother or grandmother or relative who is or was a Christian, and that their 'moral compass' is from them.

CHAPTER 7
TV and Film Production

God is seeking men and women of reckless faith today ... to be
reckless in your faith does not mean to be unthinking, but the
reverse – concentrated, single-minded in your concern that
God should be glorified and souls won.
(George Verwer, http://www.georgeverwer.com/
ip.php?tp=powerQuotes)

'Hello, my name is X and I am the senior producer for ABC
News's *20/20* TV programme with Barbara Walters.'

I was jumping up and down – at least inside – at this point.

'We are putting together an interview with a famous
international film star and we need you to help put that together
in London. Is that something you could do?' was the million-
dollar question.

'No problem at all. I will need to know who the person is to
tailor the shoot for them,' was my response.

'It's Angelina Jolie who has just finished filming the *Tomb
Raider* film,' was the unexpected reply.

'I'll work on it,' I said, with typically British understatement.

I had recently put a listing in one of the film and TV trade
publications and it seemed like my mobile phone would not stop
ringing. Most of the queries were from people attempting to get
a 'quote' which, when completed, was 90 per cent of the actual

work. When many of them did not pan out that meant a lot of man hours wasted with no results.

The day after that call, I received a number of locations for the filming and checked into permits and what was needed to make it an overwhelming success. I emailed these across to the producer and waited.

When he arrived in London, the star of *20/20* – Barbara Walters – a good friend of Angelina and a veteran of television, had her favourites and the producer himself, his. My brief was to get them over to my choice which I had previously used before. I then also learned the story behind the filming. Barbara Walters, interviewer of top celebrities and politicians including Fidel Castro, Princess Diana and many, many others, had previously interviewed Angelina. Angelina had said to Barbara that the next time Barbara interviewed her she could do it at the new home she had just bought near London. The shoot was set up but the redecoration work at the large home was delayed. This is when I was called in.

Barbara has a long association with London and has a number of friends here. Her preferred place of lodgings is the Savoy Hotel, at that time showing some signs of wear before its recent refit. Barbara wanted to do the interview at the Savoy, but my reaction was that it would definitely be too small. The producer did a recce and, sure enough, there was no chance of ever fitting the crew in that this production would entail – somewhere between ten to twenty members with monitors, cameras and lighting everywhere.

The producer's choice sounded ideal – for California. This, however, was London – in the autumn. His thought was to do the entire interview on a boat on the River Thames. I explained that the negatives were numerous: 1) This time of year, there could be a heavy mist, or rain could be pelting down, or it might be windy; 2) Wherever the boat went we would need documentation and permits from every borough we filmed in – as well as the Rivers Authorities' and, if near a bridge, from the authority over that; 3) The Thames is actually a very noisy place to film on with horns going off – sometimes just because a ship's captain sees that you are filming.

My choice, which at first met great resistance, was a pub in Notting Hill that I had used before for a major filming. The venue had a typical 'pull a pint' pub room. It also had a traditional 'back room' with games and couches. Then it had a great conservatory with some stained-glass windows. Last of all, it had an outdoor garden seating area. For my mind this offered four different locations for one price and location.

To an American, a bar is often a place for 'low lifes' where children are excluded and darkness is the order of the day. I explained to the producer that in England, a pub is more like a community centre which, nowadays, attracts families – there are play areas in many of them. It is *not* the bar of the American.

We met Barbara Walters that night at the hotel. I had grown up watching her on TV and it was actually unusual to see her in real life acting more like a Jewish grandmother than the young reporter I had first seen on the news. She was kind and caring, but with a mind for business.

After being introduced to her, her first reaction was, 'I want the Savoy.' After explaining the problems with that option, and with the producer's option, he told her about the pub. 'What – a bar?' she loudly asked. 'We're going to film *in a bar*?'. The producer, prompted by myself, explained that it was more like a community centre than a bar. She agreed that she would try it.

On the day of the filming, with just a matter of minutes to

go before the crew would start to arrive, I was at the location in Notting Hill, nowadays a favourite place to film. In fact, last year I filmed a scene next to Paddington bear in the film *Paddington 2* on Portobello Road nearby. I then received a frantic phone call that Angelina would be, for the first time on television, showing her adopted Cambodian son, Maddox. That necessitated an additional ideal location for filming with him.

Putting a London production together with just weeks to spare is a major accomplishment. Getting a last-minute location is an impossibility. But I carried it off and received all approvals for a nearby park and playground.

The producer had been in a positive frame of mind and told me that I was not needed for filming day as ABC News New York and London had it 'all in hand'. I offered to stay and take the informal photos (which I always demand to do as a favour) and, if not needed they would not have to pay me. Immediately the producer saw the error of his ways and I was back on the day's crew sheet.

The lighting men were putting up a crane with gels (coloured lighting insertions that the light goes through to give the impression of stained glass or coloured windows). This was not enough for the producer. He and I visited the quaint and quirky antique shops of Notting Hill, begging and borrowing real stained-glass windows that we would dot around the conservatory area where the interview would take place. When they said 'OK' they would then ask *me* for a £2,000 to £3,000 deposit for their precious windows. I, of course, looked at the producer. In each shop he would take out the company credit card. Remembering that ABC at that time was owned by the Walt Disney Company, I was not that shocked to see him take out, literally, a 'Mickey Mouse Credit Card' with the mouse's famous face all over it! We then lugged back each of those beautiful pieces and they were put on set.

The conservatory, of course, was round and a dolly track was laid down so that the camera could also, during the interview, film looking from the outside in. I might be prejudiced but I think it was one of the most beautiful interviews I have ever seen on national TV.

Eventually Angelina came on set and Barbara met her and spoke with her for a few minutes. Then Barbara introduced her to the son of an old friend of hers from London. Remember that Angelina was single at this time and I think that Barbara thought she could do a bit of matchmaking. We all gave the two of them some time. (At that moment there were customers in the pub. By the time we started rolling we all understood that the public would have to be asked to leave and the proceeds of the day paid for by ABC.)

I had decided to bring the DVD insert of my own copy of *Tomb Raider* and I cheekily interrupted the conversation, asking her to autograph it for me. I think one or two of the crew then also bothered her.

With everything in place, the interview began and most of us watched it in the next room where a monitor was set up. The hairdresser watched every movement to see whether or not he would be needed on set. The costume people made sure that everything was 'just right'. Everyone was looking at the filming from their own perspective. I felt like a proud 'Papa' making it all gel together.

Angelina talked about her compassion, her adopted son, her work on a film about medical personnel giving their lives for those who needed help so desperately. Barbara, in the midst of the interview, asked about her singleness. Angelina answered that she had not had sex in a few years. It was that sound bite that hit the headlines around the world. Just after the interview it was said that she received a phone call from Brad Pitt and the rest is history.

After the hour or so filming, the crew departed and Barbara wandered off. There I stood next to Angelina Jolie, alone, a bit intimidated, I must say. I must be one of the few men in the world who can say they spent about five to ten minutes alone with her! I would like to say that I said some great gems of wisdom. I prayed alone and was fully aware that on a film or TV set, unless a 'star' talks to you it means that they want to calm down and relax from the stress of it all and should be left alone with their thoughts.

Finally, everyone returned and the ABC News photographer took some shots. In between I took a few hundred – of Angelina by herself and of her with Barbara. I always like the 'in-between' unposed photographs that I take during a professional photo opp. I think that they show more of the person's character.

Eventually Barbara looked at me and said, 'Who are you?'

I wanted to say, 'We met yesterday, remember?' but thought better of that reply.

'It's OK. X (the producer) knows about the photos.'

'Well, stop it!' was Barbara's curt reply.

The producer, who I had begun to get on with quite well, gave me a nod, a 'cut it' and said, 'That's it for now, David.' Later I also got a few great shots of Barbara and Angelina and Maddox on the way to the filming at the park.

After any major shoot there always seems to be an elation and a coming down after doing something so highly stressful. Carrying onto the train my production case and a super-sized poster from *Tomb Raider*, I felt like it would be very difficult to have another job such as this. It was a great deal of work, but so many interesting contacts and learning.

Another interesting filming job was co-producing a feature for the well-known and historical Holland America cruise line. This was the company that had carried so many immigrants to America and to Ellis Island to start a new life. At one point they had, on their website, a listing of all passengers carried from the Old World. The title of the film was *The Romance of Europe* and they had already filmed portions in Denmark, France and a number of other countries. London was their final port of call. I enjoy the camaraderie that comes with a tightly knit crew.

Working with us was the producer of the film company that was making the shoot, myself and the producer from Holland America Line, a director of photography, director and others, comprising about ten to fifteen of us. Meeting them at the airport was the start of very hard work, but the culmination of months of my putting this whole leg of the journey together. We had our own minibus and I had even arranged 'American-looking actors and actresses'. My favourite choice was a man called Graham and a woman who made it through the casting to win the role.

I had done a bit of research *after* choosing Graham and discovered that he was, without my realising it, a household name. He was popular with many ITV shows. When Cilla Black hosted the popular TV show Blind Date, after each section she would say 'Our Graham, tell us about our contestants' – this was that Graham! It was quite controversial but Saturday night's favourite voice – Graham – had been axed from the show just before I contacted him. I chose Graham because he looked like a travelling American.

Phoning Graham and telling him that he had won the part, he was chuffed. This was his very first job post-*Blind Date*. I said, 'I hate to ask, but are you "Our Graham"?' He then went into 'our

Graham mode' and we had a great laugh together.

The woman that I had chosen was also a veteran TV star and had been in many programmes through the years. It was a joy to get to know them as we travelled throughout London – from Tower Bridge to the Tower of London. While filming at the Tower I could see that things were about to wrap for that location.

'If you grab your camera and tripod and follow me I am sure that you are going to get some shots that you will not believe,' I commented to the crew. As we almost ran across the bridge to the brand-new London City Hall, the crew regathered, along with hundreds of onlookers. By then we had it confirmed that the Queen would shortly be passing by. So there we were, putting into the film *The Romance of Europe* an unprecedented shot of the Queen waving at our cameras, and of her husband, Prince Philip.

On the bus our excitement exploded. Everyone was thanking me for 'arranging it' when I knew it was just God ordering my footsteps each step of the way. The Holland America Line producer phoned her husband, I think in the middle of the night, and told him that she had met the Queen of England!

After that it was difficult not to get a great recommendation. After the London filming (including hours of time lapse at the Albert Memorial) we headed to Canterbury Cathedral for some great filming followed by our final location – the cliffs of Dover.

Another of my favourite collaborations was with the Kentucky Horse Park. This is the location in America where rich and famous people go to buy champion horses for their stock. To entice and seduce buyers, the Park has a lush film. It was time for that film to be replaced by our production. Technically this was billed as a recce but, due to its depth, I would more classify it as a shoot.

The producer and director had already filmed on the plains of Dakota and a bit in the Middle East. In America the buffalos roaming and the horses there had been beautifully filmed.

The film was to tell the story of the history of *The Horse* and its role for thousands of years. Our part – in England – started at a brewery where the original draft horses were used. We got to ride on one of the horse-drawn wagons and that was a real treat. As I like to make every shoot a real experience, especially for overseas crew, I add in some surprises. On this trip, our first night was in a hotel in the picturesque village of Castle Combe. It is here that the original film of *Doctor Dolittle* was made. Antennas are banned, which is one of the reasons this town in Wiltshire is a popular choice for filming. I quite often went here, when I lived in the West Country, for Sunday afternoon tea. For filmmakers, it is like being in a visual candy store.

We went to the brewery and then two horse farms – one in the Exmoor Park and one in the Dartmoor Park. We also looked at and filmed the wild horses on the moors. It ended up being a fantastic time. We finished the recce at the polo grounds where Prince Charles used to play, and the princes. I know a man that used to do the PR and was a Christian and member of the Bible Society. He is a close friend to Prince Charles and Camilla as well as the princes. We received unprecedented permission for one of the princes to appear in the film on screen. What an amazing coup!

The sad part of the whole story is that the film company was not able to complete financing for the film. As far as I know, the film has never been produced.

I began being very choosy about contracts that I took. One South Korean producer asked me to set up filming on London Bridge – as all clients do. It takes quite a few minutes to explain to them that they actually want Tower Bridge and *not* London Bridge.

I knew a great location near the London City Hall to do some filming, with great shots in the background. That's where we filmed. Then I was told that we were to have filming on Tower Bridge. I explained that this would take weeks and a few different permits to carry off. The production company refused.

'OK,' I said. 'How many are in the shot? Any extras?'

I was told, 'Just one person and two cameras with tripods.'

'If we are going to do this shot we will do it – no tripods and have one pass, as we are without permits and just taking a chance.'

The next day arrived and I knew that I was in deep trouble. The bridge was filled with twenty to thirty extras and not the one that I had been promised. A man was putting down gaffer tape all over the bridge. Then I saw a man holding a Gideon's Bible. I thought to myself, 'Oh no! I am being employed by the Moonies! How could I do that?'

I gingerly walked up to the director and asked, 'Why is that man carrying that book?'

His reply? 'Oh, we saw that in the hotel room and liked the colour of it!'

I breathed a temporary sigh of relief.

One camera was on a tripod on one end of the bridge, and the other at the other end of the bridge. These extras walked past the cameras, dodging London commuters.

I was very animated at this point. 'You've lied to me every step of the way. This is not one or two extras and you are marking bridge property. I can see the authorities in their office on the bridge and they are calling the police. I quit!' They began to tell me that they wanted to rent the barges on the river and to immediately get a flying drone to go over the river.

'You are in too deep in this shoot and have deceived me,' I said. That is the one and only time that I walked off of a shoot and to this day I do not know how much they paid to get everyone to turn a blind eye. It was the most bizarre film shoot that I have ever been involved with.

CHAPTER 8
Into China
(2004–2013)

He is no fool who gives what he cannot keep to gain what he cannot lose.

(Missionary martyr, Jim Elliot)

After holding our *AGAPE: Live!* leadership training events and evangelistic meetings throughout Europe, as a ministry, we began to sense the leading of the Lord to bring this equipping and encouraging of global Christian leaders into closed countries.

This was a big step of faith, and our hearts began to burn towards reaching China. We sensed God saying to us these words: 'I will open up China.' Nothing more. Nothing less. I borrowed some photos from a Christian that we knew who had taken a trip into the country to carry in Bibles. That's all we had to publicise the need for prayer that we required to help us to go into one of the most closed countries to the gospel in the world. In spite of having connections and knowing Brother Andrew (Open Doors), we just held it all in prayer.

Well – I say 'prayer', but if often took the form of arguing with God. I can remember counter-arguing God's leading by saying, 'You don't understand. We have been reaching Europe via budget airlines. How could we ever reach China and the great expense that that entails?' Have you ever argued with God like that? In spite of His many miracles in our lives and ministry, we are sure that God cannot do 'even greater things'!

In the midst of this to-ing and fro-ing, I remember receiving an invitation for a very special missions conference to be held in Tokyo, Japan. I had longed to film and document the real situation there pertaining to Christianity and missions. The conference was unusual in that the percentage of people from the West invited to attend (by invitation only) was in direct proportion to the number of missionaries of sending nations. Therefore, since the West has drastically declined in the number of missionaries sent and Asia and Africa has drastically increased, very few Westerners were invited. I felt God's leading to attend, although it would be another great step of faith.

It was such an encouraging time. I think they were saying there was somewhere between 3,000 to 5,000 people each day of the conference. I kept running into people from South Korea and began to hear the exciting things that God was doing there. As I almost always do, I decided to do some filming and I received permission to be a secondary film unit at the event. A Christian Korean TV network was filming everything else.

One day a man came up to me, a Dr Cho (no, not *that* Dr Cho!). He told me that he was running a missions conference later in that year. He wanted to have a bit of talking to camera to help to promote it. I agreed to do the filming during our lunchtime. This I did and we exchanged business cards and I gave him the tape. I thought nothing more about it as there were so many people to meet – from Egypt, China, countries throughout Africa and so on.

Although we had a printed programme there did not seem to be a list of the main evening speakers. Somehow I heard, at the last minute, that Dr Young Hoon Lee, the successor to Dr David

Yonggi Cho as the senior pastor of the world's largest church, was to speak at the closing ceremony on the final evening.

On that night, before the service, I went up to the main dressing room. I had interviewed one of the leading pastors from Tokyo there so found it very easily. There was a security man on the door. With tripod and camera, I stated: 'I would like to film an interview with Dr Young Hoon Lee.' The security guard went inside, had a short conversation and then nodded for me to come into the room.

There was Dr Young Hoon Lee, pastor of the world's largest church, and next to him, a friend of his, the Dr Cho for whom I had done the favour and filmed the video clip! I understand that Dr Cho said to Dr Lee that he knew me, that I was a good guy and that Dr Lee should do it! Dr Lee then told me to return to the room at the end of the closing evening celebrations.

When I returned a few hours later, I had scribbled down some questions that I thought all of the pastors in the world would like to ask this gracious man of God. When I arrived at the door I was invited in. There, in one room, were many of the Christians VIPs from Japan and the ones from South Korea who had just been on the platform.

Dr Lee invited me to sit down and enjoy a drink and a snack. Then he said, 'Begin please!'

'Now?' I asked, bemused by the openness of Dr Lee.

'Yes,' he answered.

There, in the small dressing room with top VIPs and my camera, and another video camera from Seoul and Dr Lee's church and also an official photographer from the church, were Dr Lee and I, filming an interview that I had never dreamt in my wildest dreams would ever happen. My knees were literally shaking, knowing this awesome responsibility.

After the interview, Dr Lee gave me his business card with personal contact details and I gave him mine.

'I will be in Scotland next week. Let's have a meal together,' said the senior pastor.

'I am sorry, but I will be in another country at that time,' was my reply.

'Well, come to Seoul sometime and we will have a meal together and film another interview and I will show you around our church,' he countered.

Since that time I have had seven private meals with Dr Lee, who is always so very gracious. We trade stories about what we have been up to, and he always asks to be updated as to what is happening in the US and UK, Church-wise and spiritually. We write back and forth regularly and he always asks, when we meet, what I would like help with. We always have a few projects that we are working on together.

Jackie Pullinger MBE, author of the classic best-selling book *Chasing the Dragon* used to come to the UK very infrequently. On one of her trips I was able to interview her at the Greenbelt Festival. We seemed to get along quite well, especially after I understood her sharp wit and sometimes unexpected answers. Jackie invited me, whenever I could make it, to China and Hong Kong, to visit her work and to see their new HQ there. I put that in the *China* pigeonhole in my mind and heart.

A short time later, I had the opportunity to interview Argentinian evangelist Dr Luis Palau, and spent a few hours just chatting with him afterwards. In the course of the conversation, I mentioned that God seemed to be leading us into China. Dr Palau had just finished co-writing a book entitled *Riverside Chats: A Friendly Dialogue Between an Atheist and a Christian*. Dr Palau was the Christian, and the head of the Chinese government's

Information Agency was the atheist. The book, surprisingly, was published by the Chinese government – and was mandatory reading for secondary students in that land.

Dr Palau gave a recommendation of myself to his contacts and told them that I would be contacting them. Later, on my first visit to China, he was true to his word. Some of my best friends there I met through Dr Palau's contacts list. Besides that, I discovered a few years later that when Dr Palau gave me the contacts he also wrote personal letters to all of those men and stated that I was a good person, we are a good organisation, and can be trusted to work together. I am thankful to God for this breakthrough.

In the midst of this argument with God about China, I found myself in London in the middle of an afternoon. The free *Metro* newspapers from the morning were just thrown into the rubbish bin and never recycled. On this day there was one copy of *Metro* in the newspaper stack. I felt that that was so unusual that it must be from God. I took the copy and put it under my arm. Finally, sitting on the Underground train, I opened the newspaper and was shocked to read the headline 'Budget Airline to Fly to Hong Kong – for £58'! I said to myself, 'OK, God. You have my attention.' Reading further I saw that the airline was being started by a Christian minister from Hong Kong and would be based on 'Christian principles'. 'OK, God. You *really* have my attention!' I cried.

When I got home I looked up the airline on the internet and discovered that the founder's wife and I both graduated from the same Christian educational institution. I then filled in the online enquiry form, explaining that God had called us to begin working in China and that I knew Jackie Pullinger, and mentioned a few other names. I asked for some free airline tickets to Hong Kong to begin our work there and do the filming that we needed to complete. At first an autorepsonder came, saying 'Thank you. Your comments are noted' or words to that effect. However, a few weeks later, I received an email saying that the owner of the airline, a minister, would like to donate would like to personally give me the tickets for a flight at Christmastime for me and my family to go to Hong Kong and film whatever we needed to! What a shock and answer to prayer! After that it was so much easier to believe God's promises of His provision for our needs.

As we sat in the seats of this plane, grateful to the owners of the airline, we put on our headphones and found an entertainment channel with praise and worship music! We felt like royalty; children of the King!

Jackie Pullinger met me at the train station near her HQ in Hong Kong one day while we were there. We both filled each other in on what we had been doing – at the same time. Then, just as we entered the gates to her compound, she stopped the driver.

'Get out! Get out!' she ordered me.

She took me over to this interesting wall at the entrance to the compound. The stones were all different shapes and colours, but had been set together to blend into a beautiful array of diversity. She motioned with her finger, pointing to the stones.

'These stones we have gathered from all over Hong Kong. They are stones that the builders have rejected.' While that was sinking into my heart and soul, she continued with a message so powerful I have repeated it hundreds of times around the world. 'These are our people – rejected of men but accepted of God.'

Afterwards, I was able to interview some of Jackie's leaders. These leaders are transitory, as some come from China and other places and go back there transformed and bringing the Good News. We looked out over the hills, where the most outstanding site is a huge racetrack. I was told, 'More money is lost in one

Saturday at that racetrack than at all the racetracks in the UK in a year. Many of those people we then need to help as they look to drugs and alcohol as an answer to their problems.'

The interview took place in a lovely garden with Cantonese scriptures written in large letters scattered throughout. Later I learned that this had been Jackie's late husband's favourite spot. His ashes are buried there.

The years that I have been in and out of China have yielded some great results – in every way.

As I have already stated, about half the guests of one of the series, *Principles of Business*, are from businesses in China. That has led to some wonderful openings there. China's top fashion designer and her husband (designing for Rihanna and Lady Gaga, the Beijing Olympics, top Chinese film and TV stars and even the wife of China's president) said, when I interviewed her, 'Let's make this about a friendship and not just about an interview.' (That is something echoed by a number of our guests.) So, following the Chinese custom for building friendships, in many of my trips we meet together for a meal. We talk about Buddhism, Christianity, life, death, kids, education – and I can be salt and light. Many doors have been opened for other connections and I am still working through those.

On one trip I interviewed a man who is related to the last emperor of China. I next interviewed one of the country's top economists, who has an amazing testimony. The third on that trip was a man who stated, in the daily communist newspaper, that China should accept the Underground Church as a powerful force for good in the country. When I told a key contact for China about these three men that I had interviewed, he said, 'Do you realise that you interviewed the top three Christian leaders in China today?' My footsteps are led by God.

I try to film the stories of very unusual businesses that make China such an exciting place. On one trip I interviewed a man who calls himself Gunter and has put together the Central Perk Café – at the top of an office block in central Beijing! You would think that you were on the set of the popular TV series, *Friends*. While there I learned that the TV series is important to young Chinese people because it is how many of them learned English!

On another trip I interviewed an Iranian Brit who is one of the world's foremost experts on the Beijing (Peking) opera. He often performs in some of the larger productions. Our interview was filmed in a park where, in the background, we could hear someone also performing some of this unique entertainment.

I meet regularly with both previous and new contacts and keep their identity secret. I help to identify trends in the Christian Church in the West and where I see it headed. It has been amazing to have started to come to China when it was on the rise, and seeing it become the world leader in economy and business that it is.

CHAPTER 9
North Korea
(2013–15)

No one has the right to hear the gospel twice, while there
remains someone who has not heard it once.
(Missionary pastor of The Peoples Church, Toronto,
Oswald J. Smith)

'What would be the most impossible thing that I could do?' I
sensed God asking me one day. I believe that prayer is more
than just bowing and kneeling, but is a constant freeway of
communication between God and myself.

I don't know how to describe how I hear God's voice. It has
never been audible. It's just an inner witness and phrase or
sentences that come. I quite often reply to this voice. It has taken
years of following God when and where He leads – no matter
how foolish it sometimes seems. Sometimes I know specifically
why I was called to a certain place or to do a certain thing. More
often than not, I do *not know*. It could be that He is just looking
for my obedience or it could be something that I will *never* know
until eternity!

I replied to what I believed to be God's question. 'I would have
to say that it would be, open the doors to North Korea as 1) That's
an impossibility and 2) I do not know anyone there or who works
there.'

I left it at that.

One time at the start of one of my private meals with Dr Young Hoon Lee, he asked me, 'What would you like? Would you like to reach North Korea?'

'Oh, yes,' I replied quickly. 'We really sense that the Lord is opening up that nation.'

Some months later I filmed an interview with Lord David Alton, a Christian and also the head of the All-Party Parliamentary Group for North Korea. After the interview we talked at length, mostly about North Korea. Because his purpose there was to push for humanitarian rights I did not sense that that would be the way forward.

I still awaited that 'peace and joy' for the door that I really sensed was from God.

After preaching at an international church in China, the pastor invited me to lunch the next day. He was Korean, Uzbekhi and Russian! Over lunch I felt led to share with him that I was feeling God's leading to begin working in North Korea but I knew no one there.

'You need to meet my friend X,' he surprisingly answered. 'He runs four bakeries in the country through his charity.' (There are now six.)

I almost jumped up in excitement. 'Where do I need to go to meet X?' I asked, blurting out the words.

'That's easy,' the pastor replied. 'He lives in London!'

This angle of work in North Korea – the humanitarian side – seemed to fit like a jigsaw puzzle piece.

Back in the UK I met with this man at a McDonald's. He was a man of great works but few words. 'I am leaving for North Korea on (a certain date) and you can come along,' he offered.

Wow! What joy and excitement filled my heart and soul that

once again, God had made a way.

I soon discovered that the charity was entirely run by volunteers. The founder spends much of his time in one of the Koreas and also in Beijing – exactly where I had been going for almost a decade, at that time. I soon discovered that Beijing is, in many ways, the gateway to North Korea. A direct flight from Beijing to Pyongyang sets you down, via its own airline, right in the heart of the country!

I met him again in Beijing and we took a taxi to the North Korean Embassy. When I saw where I was in relation to the places in Beijing that I knew, I realised that it was directly across the street from what, through the years, had been one of my favourite places to eat – outside in the summer – and when I had, I had often looked at the building across the street. I had *never* realised that it was the North Korean Embassy!

Stepping foot inside the embassy you *know* that you are not just in another country but in the midst of another mind-set. A large floor-to-ceiling painting shows The Great Leader and Our Dear Leader as I grew to learn how to refer to the father and the grandfather of the current leader, Kim Jong-un.

Instead of the swish China visa office in London you have a very no-nonsense table in the middle of the floor, and a counter. Simplicity is a necessity in things relating to the North Korean government, as nothing is to be wasted on bureaucratic furnishings.

Amazingly, within a matter of minutes, there was a North Korean visa in my hands – something I actually thought I would never see – not that I ever, in my wildest imagination, ever thought about going into North Korea, for *any* reason.

The days counted down until it was time to catch a flight to the world's most unknown and, some say, brutal country in the world. When travelling into NK, we leave literally almost everything behind! No business cards, no surplus electronics and, as a rule, we just travel with a carry-on piece of luggage so that the checked-in allowance can be used to bring in some toys and treats for the kids in the schools. Every kilogram counts!

The Koryo airline check-in desk is in a distant part of the Beijing Airport. Standing in line with us was one of the most curious collection of people. It reminded me of a flight I took into Nairobi, where everyone on the plane was either a relief worker, a minister or a worker with some sort of charity.

At the front of our queue was a man that I felt at the time that I should get to know but did not, at that point. He and his group of about six had so many equipment cases and boxes that I thought the plane would be full of just their gear. Trying to eavesdrop and find out where they were from and what they were doing, I heard the man in charge of it all introduce the man next to him. 'This is the world's foremost expert on TB,' he said. I later learned that the head of this large charity does tremendous work in giving treatment to fight TB. The man's father had started about fifty Christian hospitals in South Korea. When Billy Graham came into North Korea, he had been his translator. (This I learned from the internet, not from overhearing.)

To my right were a couple of young men explaining how in North Korea, as in China, you cannot be a journalist or media person and get into the country.

Going to the departure lounge for our flight into Pyongyang, we started talking in very hushed tones as we knew that in all probability some of the people on the flight would be North Korean government workers. In my heart I had that feeling of 'this could be my last time alive and living in freedom'. It's things like that that play on your mind during your stay. The other sense is that you will not, for the whole time there, actually say what you think, or show any expression of surprise or shock.

When our flight was called, we walked to the plane. I had already learned that the airline bought retired Aeroflot plane stock when they had outlived their usefulness. This did not fill me with any confidence. Aboard the plane I began to see the North Korean persona. There is a high level of the appearance of wealth and beauty. Each of the North Korean stewardesses were some of the most beautiful women I have ever seen. However, scratching beneath the surface, you could notice that again, not much money was put into the frill of flying and appearing that one is in a five-star hotel in the sky. The word I could think of was 'utilitarian'.

I had already read in someone's report that we would be handed an English copy of the *Pyongyang Times* with, always, the photograph of Kim Jong-un on it doing and inspecting something. From what I read, if you fold or throw away the newspaper or deface the photograph, that is a serious, punishable offence.

We passed over some of the most beautiful landscape and I would have loved to film it all. I had taken along a small consumer HD camera to film as much as I was allowed to, which was not that much compared to my other trips. No broadcast cameras were allowed here, or any association with journalism.

As they began to bring our meal, I watched as each row unwrapped their hamburgers and thought to myself, 'That is a nice change, having a hamburger. I am really looking forward to that.' The greenish, brown material inside we still have not identified – whether animal, vegetable or mineral.

Watching the TV screens I was amused by seeing, for the first time, North Korean cartoons. Here was a plane full of business people and very high-level professionals, and we were being fed a diet of whimsical cartoons. Later I learned that these home-grown characters have nearly cult status with children throughout that nation. The content I found quite interesting in such a communist-styled country. The story, from what I could figure, was of a lone boy/animal who succeeded only on his own. The crowds were all wrong and inept. In a nation where following the crowd is required, I found that to be an unusual message. Many things about North Korean films baffled me, and I would love to research more about their history sometime.

We landed at an airport under construction. Everything was laid out like a large hangar with desks and glass windows everywhere. We seemed to go from pillar to post to get our paperwork stamped and scrutunised. Anything considered dangerous must be declared. For example, the charity founder always brings in his Bible and that must be taken out and shown to the authorities. On leaving, it must be shown again and ticked off on a special form. Suitcases and boxes are X-rayed and mobile phones taken, their details recorded.

Finally we were through – alive and in one piece! Our *minders* met us – on this trip there being a total of five! My translator was a woman. I was placed in one car and X in another. The reason given later was that my 100kg-plus weight was too much for one car… My own thoughts are that I needed to be cross-examined. Some weeks before the trip I had to give details about myself, a copy of my identification, my CV for the last so many years. In cases like this I have a CV of the 'tent-making' work that I have done through the years (non-media and non-Christian). The driver in my car, I learned later, appeared to be quite high-ranking. Getting a position to spend time with foreigners is a great privilege. You eat as Westerners eat (even more so, I would say) and get to live the high life. You also have to be greatly trusted. I have been told that there are at least two minders at all times with Westerners. They are both from different jurisdictions and always have the notebooks typical of North Koreans. They report everything done by us and also report on each other. Someone has told me that they are armed in case one of the two tries to defect.

Being in North Korea for the first time and not having X with me in the car, was unnerving to say the least. I was constantly grilled – in a seemingly nice way – about my work and employment history. 'You have worked for a villa company?' I was quizzed. (One of my tent-making jobs was doing the PR and marketing for a luxury villa company.)

'Yes!' I answered abruptly, not wanting to elaborate.

There was almost a childish look in the eyes of my minder. 'What's a villa?'

It then dawned on me that this was not just a different ideology, but a whole new world. There is no internet for 99 per cent of the population. I am told that there is what can only be called a national intranet of propaganda and information that is 'allowed' to be accessed by some students and higher-level workers. You cannot phone outside of the country, in spite of there being so many mobile phones. As far as everyone was concerned, I was incommunicado until my return from NK – a bit like the astronauts when they used to be on the dark side of the moon.

'And what is a motel? And a shopping mall?' The questions were now coming thick and heavy. 'You are a marketing consultant?'

'Yes.'

'Good. What's a marketing consultant?'

After explaining the work of a typical marketing consultant, being careful to avoid any media involvement, my minder turned to me and said, 'Marketing consultant. I think I would like to be one here in North Korea.'

The roads from the airport to the hotels for Westerners are about ten lanes – five on each side and nicely paved. They are all straight and pass by some of the most famous monuments, usually having to do with *Unification and Peace*. I started to get the impression that I was actually on a film set as everything and everywhere was all calculated to give a certain impression. As we finally entered the heart of Pyongyang I began to notice the lack of traffic lights. In their place were, again, some of the most beautiful women I have seen, in blue uniforms, directing the traffic. At every intersection they were there.

Normally by now, coming from the airport I would have taken hundreds of photographs. Yet every photo was scrutinised and, I began to find, the look in the rear-view mirror of the man I thought to be just the driver, controlled whether my minder cautioned me or allowed me (not very often) to photograph.

I once attempted to take a photo of people waiting for a bus. 'That is not allowed!' I was sternly told.

Since I knew my minder a bit more by then, I asked, 'Why ever not?'

'People would get the wrong impression' – something I was told over and over and over again.

'What? That people must wait for buses? That happens in every city around the world!' I quipped.

In the middle of one trip when I was testing out the limits of what I could get away with, my minder asked me, 'Are you trying to get me killed?' This is a phrase that we jokingly use in the West quite often. I laughed and then realised that she was not joking.

We finally arrived at the Western *allowed* hotel near a huge concert hall and just around the corner from the newspaper office. On the front of it were the well-lit, day and night, photos of *The Great Leader* and *Our Dear Leader*, both of them considered gods. The present leader, it would seem, is still under probation as I would call it and has not yet received divine status.

The hotel was over 100 years old and had previously been a Japanese hotel. In the lobby, as in all public buildings, were floor-to-ceiling portraits of *Our Great Leader* and *Our Dear Leader*. In schools, the portraits portray them holding children. In factories dealing with produce, they are holding fruit and smiling – always smiling! Flowers are always placed in huge vases next to the giant paintings.

One can never leave the hotel alone, without a minder, as that would be an imprisonable offence for both yourself and your minders. The lobbies are large and there always seems to be minders waiting for their clients. To the side I noticed a little shop that I would return to in order to get a supply of water.

The room, I was told in a whisper by X, was bugged. We were not sure if there were cameras also. Daily, we understood, our suitcases were gone through and the rubbish bins searched. The view was great outside my window, and I began to notice older people on their haunches (something also common in China), cutting the grass using scissors – one of the most common foods is grass soup. Outside in the car park you could see the cars of the Westerners' minders.

The bathroom was basic and hot water, at least in this hotel, ran only at certain hours. Towels were more like tea towels in England and the soap was a very basic form. Having the amenity of a toothbrush and toothpaste, I decided to use this on my trip. Although very unusual-tasting, it did the work.

Going downstairs, under the watchful eye of at least one of the minders, I bought some water and a bag of crisps – one of the few provisions in pretty much the only shop I would see on the whole trip – *not* the one souvenir shop. For some reason North Korea does not want you having any of their currency. In Pyongyang you can use Euros or Chinese money, while in the north it was only Chinese money. In one shop, with a smile, after I realised the shop worker was having trouble finding the right Euros for my change, I said, 'You can give it to me in North Korean money if you would like.' I was either ignored or she was unable to answer me.

On the landing between floors was a smallish souvenir shop. There were dozens of titles of books by *The Great Leader* and *Our Dear Leader* on various subjects from the history of the world to war to life in general. There were North Korean flags, and some small trinket-type handmade varieties of bookmarks. My choice was the lovely embroidered simple artwork of the North Korean women in their local costumes.

Every morning at around 6am we developed a habit of walking along the river with one of our minders. We had a bit more freedom to take photos, most of the time. One morning there was a group of about fifty, mostly women, dancing in a ballroom manner. The music was lovely, in a Chinese style, and seemed to be very romantic. Some of the women had a look on their faces that seemed to speak of loves that once were. When I asked what the lyrics were to this one song which seemed to get the ladies swooning, it was along the lines of 'Oh, our Great Leader. He is our everything. It is his praises that we sing. He is our life.' Now those looks almost seemed incongruous and much beyond hero worship.

Back on the road, the streets continued to be, in the environs of Pyongyang, ten lanes, however, unpaved. Along the way, little old ladies threw piles of dirt on the potholes. The roads were littered with broken-down trucks, sometimes needing a new tyre. Because there were no 'spares and repairs', the men were jacking up the vehicles with whatever was handy and being inventive on how to fix the tyre or engine or whatever the malady was.

I can remember on one of our morning walks, thousands of bicycles were passing us on the pathway on their way to work. One or two men stationed themselves there and offered bicycle tyre repair. I thought that that was one of the most inventive things that I had ever seen.

On the trip we visited our charity's bakeries and about ten of the schools that the charity's bread and fresh soy milk is brought to. The children were, for the most part, stone-faced, and their eyes seem to show a hollowness, a sadness and an emptiness inside. I realised that, most likely, none of these children had ever seen themselves. I took my small viewfinder and continued to film but allowed the kids to see themselves. Suddenly they were the same silly and laughing children that I have seen worldwide. They poked each other and revelled in the fact that that was who they were! It was so difficult to tear ourselves away from each classroom.

In each school the children put together performances of wonderful acrobatics, singing, the playing of traditional instruments and other items which were so thrilling to watch. Those who do the best in music can go on to the most prestigious University in Pyongyang and lead a better life than many of their countrymen.

On all the trips that I have taken to document our work (I now serve on the board of the charity) they have been so eye-opening. On one trip I was graciously taken to two areas of North Korea that no Westerner has ever visited. The children, at first, looked at me with fear and curiosity. After my viewfinder trick, they again warmed to me and to our visit.

In many parts of the country the scenery is breath-taking. Visiting a dam that connects two vital part of the country, and that was built over many years, was such an insight regarding the size of many of the national projects. I look forward to revisiting and watching the progress of our work there, as now we have six bakeries helping to feed 25,000 children each day. It is one of the most heart-warming and touching projects that I think anyone could be part of – and we are in the midst of it all.

CHAPTER 10
Cambodia: Killing Fields and Living Fields (2015)

Cultivate a heart of love that knows no anger.
Old Cambodian proverb

I can still remember when the conference in Cambodia was first mentioned. It seemed so distant time-wise and also like a totally different civilisation. As the days approached and I was able to find a route to get to Phnom Penh, it was becoming more of a reality. 'How had this come about?' I asked myself.

I was asked to share a bit of my story at an international church in Beijing. At the last moment I was asked to switch Sundays as a guest singer was coming in to share. I promptly asked if I could interview him. It was then I did my research. The man that I was about to interview was actually a Messianic singer, Joshua Aaron, Jewish and from America. I had, unknowingly, been listening to his music over and over again in the car for months. The event was going to be a China Israel appreciation day and a momentous event. After my interview with Joshua Aaron, I asked if they would like me to film the concert the next day. The answer was, 'Yes!'

So there I was preparing my camera to film an unexpected concert. I was introduced to the American couple who had made it all possible – Ed and Sherry Benish – in whose heart a love for

Israel ran deeply. Sherry started talking to me about a pastor's conference in Cambodia in the summer and asked if I would like to come. I told her that she would need to send me an email so I would not forget, and that I would indeed pray about coming.

I had forgotten all about it when an email arrived from the couple. After much prayer, they had felt genuinely led of the Lord to ask me to be the first speaker invited to the conference. What an honour! I accepted totally by faith. Here I was now, on my way to that conference!

The first destination to change planes was Bangkok, Thailand. There was just enough time in the schedule to take a train and get to see a bit of the renowned city. The train from the airport was fast and a bit less crowded than London and other cities. It was hot and humid as I walked down the elevated walkway down into Bangkok itself. Getting my bearings was a bit more difficult than a typical city, so I decided to take a Tuk Tuk. Riding in what I would call a modified bicycle has its ups and downs. Being so close to polluted traffic and access to those who could easily reach out and do harm means that you are always on your guard. Actually, being in this unique means of transport is greater for taking ground-level photos but, again, the crime element means that you don't always want to be hanging out of the side of a Tuk Tuk with a phone or camera.

The historical and beautiful temples and buildings were even more overwhelming than I could imagine. In my mind there are particular cultures and places that I travel to that bring me face-to-face with the reality of a different type of life entirely. The first time in Beijing, China, the first time in Tokyo, Japan, the first time in North Korea and here – the first time in Bangkok – brought a sense of awe and wonder that is so often missing when you travel so much.

My plan was to go to the palace, walk around and then have a bite to eat next to the river – on the other side – overlooking the palace. The heat won out! I had to buy something to drink, then some quick photos and selfies and then more to drink. Thank goodness for a Portakabin style of toilet in this heavy tourist area.

I had to watch my time as well as energy levels when still suffering from jet lag. Every single building was an eye-opening insight into the long history of this nation. I tried to imagine the scenes from the film *The Beach* and other movies that glamorise the serene and peaceful settings and locations in the areas less travelled. I could imagine someone quickly jettisoning Bangkok's hectic hustle and bustle for a week or two on the beach. But I had no sense of going somewhere to relax.

Just walking along the length of the palace walls in immense heat was a workout. I decided to err on the side of caution, take some photos and then a Tuk Tuk back to the train station and train back to the airport to wait in more comfortable – and air-conditioned – surroundings. As I do in each city, I prayed for it, its people, its Christians and churches and unreached and for the nation and its leaders and government.

Theoretically, I have always taught that prayer transcends time and space. Jesus sent God's Word and it healed many who were not present. We can pray for the cities and nations of the world. Yet, I have come to appreciate more and more and see the value of actually *being* in a place and praying for its people and its leaders, churches and government. I now spend a day at least every week or ten days prayer-walking and talking to people in Borehamwood – England's Hollywood – and also Golders Green.

As I walk through London, Paris, Rome, Bangkok, Beijing, Tokyo, I am also quoting the scripture that says that *wherever my feet go, God has given it to me.* (see Deuteronomy 11:24; Joshua

1:3). For a number of years before moving to the UK I would walk through almost every area of London that I could, and pray through the streets. Years later God seemed to open up those areas for ministry. I used to pray outside of the historical BBC studios in Elstree and now God has opened those doors on a regular basis to work and pray – from the inside! In fact, I try to, at least once a year, spend time inside all of the major film and TV studios of Britain and pray for the productions, cast, crew, production companies and storylines.

Walking up the steps to the train station I found a little kiosk of a certain burger company and enjoyed a nice fish sandwich and a frozen fizzy drink – something which I enjoyed in America and whenever I see it overseas, but sadly lacking in the UK. The ride back to the airport was fast – too fast to enjoy a leisurely peek at another side of Bangkok. Finally, after a short wait, my flight was on its way to Phnom Penh, Cambodia.

Growing up, I was on the verge of being called up for *the draft*. Thankfully, my draft was deferred due to the fact that I entered college in 1970. Each year I would watch the news, the killing, the bombs, the helicopters and the devastation of Vietnam, Cambodia and the surrounding areas. I knew the Phnom Penh of the TV news and the film *The Killing Fields*. To actually be flying into this infamous area was a little unnerving and I entered with a bit of trepidation.

At the airport a seemingly very young and friendly pastor met me. From there my luggage was taken, and I clambered aboard a large Tuk Tuk along with the pastor and driver. Late at night speeding through the city on a glorified bicycle was like being caught up in a whirlwind. I saw some monuments and the palace and then, shortly afterwards, we turned into a side street. Although now about 2am, I checked into the hotel that definitely gave the impression of being in colonial days. Net curtains and old fans were everywhere.

This hotel which I had found online at discounted price I now have as my world's favourite hotel. I had wanted something set back from the busy-ness of the city and where I could prepare for my upcoming messages at the pastors' conference outside Phnom Penh. This fitted the bill perfectly. It seemed that I was upgraded to a suite of rooms. One had couches, chairs, a table and all of the luxuries one could want. The bedroom had a huge four-poster bed with mosquito-net curtains. Outside there was even a double patio – enough to house a whole army, one would think. When I asked the history of the building, I was told that it used to be the home of the mother of the king – being in such proximity to the palace.

I found Phnom Penh to be quite an interesting city, and explored it as much as I could. One day I went to a very luxurious mall and drank in the view, watching what seemed to be the upper class of Cambodia as they bought designer clothes and enjoyed Western foods and takeaways. Another day I went to a market teeming with scents and sounds, trinkets and treasures.

To me, walking through areas of shopping from both ends of the price range, helps me to understand a culture – that and the TV. In the beautiful building housing the market, I could imagine that during the war, this was probably used for something quite different. I stopped to buy a DVD about *The War* (which I must admit I still have not sat down and watched).

I had seen a flier in the hotel about a Cambodian dance night and found that to be an interesting peek into this culture. I took a Tuk Tuk to the venue – a cultural centre just around the corner from the palace. At night the tourists were gone from the area and it turned into a nightmare of a setting, but a very eye-opening one. As I stood at the gate of the cultural centre, a small naked boy was running around. A woman was trying to alternately chase him away and catch him. She just wanted him out of there. I decided to walk over to the palace and saw dozens of people sleeping in makeshift lean-tos and tents, begging for money from anyone passing by.

Across the street I went to buy some water for the performance and found a very ingenious collection of business/charity ventures. The first was a gift items shop with homemade pocketbooks, wallets, hats, purses and so on – many of them made out of discarded newspapers. The shop was run by a charity that helped the street children of Phnom Penh. Next to it was a restaurant that employed the homeless and people in need of work.

In many ways Phnom Penh is a worldwide centre of aid for the thousands of destitute people living there. Some of the dumps even have children living in them and off them. Sadly there are also con artists using work with the needy of Phnom Penh as a way to steal millions in donations!

The cultural dance evening was lovely and showed folk dancing through the years in the country. It was still tough to shake the visions of what I had seen before the performance, though. Meeting most of the performers afterwards, I learned of their dedication to bring this area of Cambodia's good history to this generation.

On the Sunday I was privileged to share God's Word at the young pastor's church, and at a prayer gathering of churches from across Phnom Penh in the evening. I must say that I am very excited when I get to spend time with young, on-fire pastors and church and ministry leaders in difficult areas and countries. I always attempt to encourage them in their work and pray for whatever needs they are facing at the moment. God is doing mighty works in places that few, if any, ever hear about.

One of my long-lasting memories was to ride on the back of the pastor's little motor scooter as we rode to my next meeting through the chaotic streets and traffic of Phnom Penh.

In my life I have visited the very sad places such as Birkenau and Auschwitz where the apple of God's eye and other outcasts were treated so inhumanely. As the Nazis wanted to destroy all evidence of their cruelty, the victims were first gassed and then burned. Their ashes, too numerous to ship out, actually became part and parcel of the land on which the slaughterhouses stand. If it is at all possible, I found that visiting the Killing Fields was even more heart-wrenching. There are actually hundreds of *killing fields* where it is estimated over 1.5 million people were cruelly murdered. The most famous one, outside of Phnom Penh, is a gruesome display of how deep and dark the mass murders were. I visited just after rainy season. At that time of year the actual cloth, bones and teeth of the victims begin coming to the surface. Signs all over the five-acre or so site tell you not to walk on them, but this is an impossibility. In a central prayer tower, hundreds of skulls and bones are piled up in a type of memorial.

It was explained by our guide that the government did not want to waste the meagre price of a bullet on the victims. Thus they would take palm tree branches apart until they exposed a lethal sword-like stem and it is these that were used to mortally wound. In a seemingly peaceful field, thousands of innocent children were murdered. Location after location speaks of the cruelty and utter disregard for human life that these men and women had. Sobering – even now as I remember the scene there. Going back to my hotel after that was a welcome relief. Every morning I enjoyed a free breakfast which included pancakes or French toast, a fruit dish, and fresh squeezed fruit juices all set next to the luxurious and inviting swimming pool. What an idyllic setting for the most reasonable price I have ever paid! I love when God allows me to both abound and be abased as He reminds me that He is our source!

The day of departure arrived and I was sitting in one of the poolside lounges behind the peaceful gate of the small compound. The hosts of the conference were so shocked that such a wonderful place existed in Phnom Penh.

Boarding a minibus with about fifteen or more people on board – all our speakers –was quite an experience. A pastor friend, Joseph, originally from Chicago but a church-planter from Beijing, sat next to me. There we were, travelling to the conference camp location in an air-conditioned bus with WiFi. For the first time in my life I was introduced to the social media app Periscope. Joseph hosted an impromptu interview with me on it and people from around the world watched as we travelled to the conference and chatted!

The conference site was a camp built by some American Christians who had set up a number of these camps and Bible schools to train up leaders for Jesus Christ. Although more fundamental than charismatic, we were hosted wonderfully and the anointing of the Holy Spirit flowed in each meeting. In one of my sessions I had been asked to share my life story, and many were blessed by it, and by knowing that God answers prayer and that He leads and guides our footsteps.

Towards the end of the conference, with over 800 pastors and church leaders in attendance, we had a very touching foot-washing service. All of the speakers took a towel and washed the feet of those servants of God present. It was a very humbling experience. This has become a very important part of this now annual conference in different locations. Some of the pastors cry as we all pray and as we wash the feet of these saints of God working in difficult situations.

Throughout the conference, leaders came up and talked about different aspects of the story that I shared. They each asked for prayer – *and* the inevitable selfie. I, myself, tried to take photos with them, but begin to lose track after the first 100 or so. Prayer services begin around 5 or 6am and the last session runs well past midnight.

On the last evening in Cambodia, our hosts put us up in a hotel in Phnom Penh so that we could catch our early flights the next morning. There were three of us men in our room, but two of us did not go with the others for a meal. My pastor friend from Beijing had invited me to meet a man who, underground, had planted over 10,000 churches across the country. He recommended we meet at a restaurant that he had frequented for years. What a joy to, again, hear what God was doing in a dangerous, difficult but rewarding work.

We arrived back in the room, but the third man had not yet arrived. About 1am he showed up and wanted to chat! Yet out of that chat a friendship grew, and I was asked to return to his home city where he ministered, Bangkok, and share with leaders at a conference there! His 3am wake-up call for an early flight did not go down very well.

While we met with the underground leader and his wife at one restaurant, almost all of the other speakers had gone to a restaurant and experience that I had recommended to them. The Foreign Correspondents Club, Phnom Penh, I had heard and read about when a teen. It smelled of intrigue and colonialism, backroom chatter and gossip, an oasis far from home in the midst of a living battlefield. When you walk upstairs into the restaurant of this fascinating venue, you are stepping back in time. Earlier in the week I had discovered it. Sitting by the large open window overlooking the Mekong River, I had sat and had an enjoyable lunch while watching tourists and fishing boats on the river, and Phnom Penh traffic going by in the street below. A pool table and piano were there as well as a vista that showed both the beauty and dereliction of architecture of a city that I grew to love.

When our hosts had booked hotel rooms for us it was lower-scale, because of the cost. A mix-up meant that we were placed in a four-star hotel instead. Our last morning breakfast before our flight was totally awesome. Breakfast was served in that hotel on the rooftop which overlooked Phnom Penh. I sat and looked at the beauty that crossed between God-made and man-made – another city that needs to know Jesus Christ as Lord!

CHAPTER 11
A Three-Nation Missionary Journey:
1 & 2 – Cyprus and Lebanon
(2016)

God uses men who are weak and feeble enough to lean on him.
(Hudson Taylor, missionary to China)

In 2016, finances began to be quite tight, even after much prayer and seeking God as to how to make up the shortfall. Most ministries and charities had been feeling the pinch for years, but since we operate with almost all volunteers – except our part-time bookkeeper – there were few places to cut back. One or two situations had come up and a couple of our major donors felt the desire to pull their support without notice. I was trying to juggle a conference that I needed to attend in Cyprus, some filming, an interview and a dual training national event in Ethiopia. Our bookkeeper had suggested that each time I combine trips (like South Korea, North Korea and China) there was a flight savings involved. Yet I could not see how it would be physically and earthly possible to combine the Middle East and Africa into one trip. But I did anyway! On top of all of this, I began to use an airline which necessitated a plane change in the heart of the Middle East.

The first stop was Cyprus. I tend to allow myself to start each trip with a free day, allowing some extra rest to get used to jet lag and any incidental filming that needs to take place. Another thing is that once a trip begins, I need fluids and juices to top me up, instead of paying hotel prices for that. On this trip I had mentioned on social media that I would be in Cyprus. A man that I had never met (to my knowledge) but who I had good mutual-friend connections with asked if I would be interested in speaking at an event where he would invite as many of the Cyprus churches and leaders as possible – on my free day.

The heart of our ministry has always been to get churches cooperating with each other. When we first started our *AGAPE*, then our *AGAPE: Live!* weekend training sessions, we stipulated that there must be at least two churches working in conjunction with each other before we would make concrete plans. In Italy we heard that two pastors who had not been getting along both arrived at the same time. They very uncomfortably greeted each other. One said, 'This is ridiculous. We must put a stop to this division and hostility towards each other and our churches. Let us make peace.' I love things like that that can bring God's people together physically, as we are already one in the Spirit!

I landed at the airport close to the ocean as the sun was just rising, and it made a beautiful background to this whole gruelling trip! Upon arriving at my hotel I went to find somewhere to have lunch, as it would be a long day. Normally before a meeting where I preach, I will fast. In this case the 40 degree (Celsius) heat and the jet lag and 3am wake-up call all combined, in my mind, to necessitate some kind of lunch. Immediately across from the hotel, I found an American-style restaurant with very few people in it. I still remember that relaxing time praying, reading over my notes for my message that evening, and watching people. I always enjoy getting to know a new culture or location by watching the people and attempting to hear what they are talking about, listening to, watching or playing! It gives me insight as to what most people's priorities are in life.

I think that a note about languages would be appropriate here, as southern Cyprus speaks Greek while the northern part (what some call *occupied*) is Turkish. I have always hated studying languages. At one point I was considering going into the medical profession and being a missionary doctor – complementing my sister's vision to be a missionary nurse. At the time it was a prerequisite to study Latin. So that is exactly what I did – for four years – being the *only* student in the class, taught by the headmistress! During some of those years her husband, the school president, was deathly ill and necessitated her taking time off. That meant that I had to study the *Gallic Wars* on my own – a tough slog even at the best of times. For two of the years I also studied French and even, for a day, took a class in German, memorising a dialogue that no German-speaking person to this day understands!

In college I took another two years of French. But it was a difficult time, due to my distaste for languages. After graduating and then working at the college, I was able to take one free course, so audited a Biblical Greek course, as I mentioned earlier. I then studied it on my own as I studied the Bible, often from a Greek New Testament, and using a Strong's Greek and Hebrew dictionary. This led to my interest in learning Russian which I saw as an impossible task. Yet, the Greek origins of Russian made it easier to understand. When I first stepped foot in that nation I had at least a rudimentary understanding of the alphabet and a number of words. Today I would say my languages would be English, French, Russian, Greek and some words of Mandarin Chinese. I am still trying to master that language!

Late afternoon approached and my friend James arrived to

take me to the meetings. We had much to talk about due to mutual friends, similar theology, interests and a love of God and His Word. We finally arrived at the venue, a nice-sized church, and found that almost 100 per cent of those in attendance were leaders. After having worked for years in Greece, I understand the hesitancy of leaders 'selling' an event until they understood it fully, its theology and purpose, and were sure that the speaker was not a wolf!

This situation worked to great advantage. First of all, many of the leaders had asked me to share some of my stories. I always find that it encourages people about being obedient to God's lifelong calling and our daily walk as He orders our footsteps.

Secondly, when leaders gather together, you are able to personally minister to them at a level with which you are not able to with 'the sheep' present. They are usually hesitant to let their guard down and balk at the very idea of people hearing what they want prayer for afterwards!

I had brought some copies of my booklet, *The Great Shepherd* (which has now been translated into ten to fifteen languages, including Spanish, Italian, Greek, Russian and Polish). These I gave out to those who were interested.

My forty-five minutes seemed like just a few minutes, as I could sense that almost everyone there was receiving from the Lord what He had, I felt, sent me to share. Afterwards I could not believe the geographical cross-section of people who came up for prayer for a variety of situations. Some of the people were from closed areas of the Middle East and at a loss as to where God wanted them next and what to do. They were a precious collection of brothers and sisters in Christ, and I look forward to the day when I will be able to return and take it all to another level.

Some say that my calling is prophetic, some say more pastoral and more say that I am a teacher of the great depths of God's Word, but in a very simple and easy to understand way. I've never been a person hung up on which 'pigeonhole' to place myself. I believe that the apostle Peter acted pastorally, evangelistically and prophetically. I believe that God has certain seasons and certain situations in which, if we are unimpressed by our own titles, He wants to use us in humble ways to do great things for Him!

We, as a ministry and producers, have provided some unique materials for airing in Arabic on SAT-7. I have also interviewed its visionary founder, Dr Terry Ascott. He is a very humble man of God, yet has accomplished what I see as one of the greatest understated works of God today. SAT-7 is a collection of five TV networks working throughout the Middle East bringing the life-changing gospel message. Their children's network is, in some places in the Middle East, one of the most popular children's TV networks. *That* is a miracle! Refugees stuck in poverty can put their children in front of the TV tuned into SAT-7 knowing that they are not going to be indoctrinated with jihadist materials, but life-building and life-changing productions teaching about the Bible and the challenges of being a young person in what can often be a violent culture.

I have attempted to attend the special, high-security conference each year, held in the Middle East. Being the special twenty-fifth anniversary of its founding, the event was held in Cyprus, where its offices are based. They gave us attendees an opportunity to see the offices and to visit some of the studios there.

To me, one of the great benefits of the conference is meeting with the underground and above-ground leaders and media people from across the Middle East, and also to meet with the wonderful supporters of the visionary work. I love it when people come on board in cooperation when there is only vision, totally by faith. In one of our church plants, we had the vision of a building. I could see the vision and dream in our members' eyes and hearts when we did not know where or what that would be – a place for us to be able to meet so many needs in so many ways. Eventually, when we bought our building, a different set of people came in. Sometimes they wanted stained-glass windows and air conditioning – not realising that just having that place was a major miracle!

At the SAT-7 conference this particular year, I was able to interview Marianne, a Lebanese-born singer and children's TV presenter. At that time she was pregnant with her son. She graciously found the time to be interviewed and to share about her life as a Christian singer in the Middle East. Her husband hosts another TV show and is also a singer and musician.

Another exciting part of the conferences are trips to see nearby areas or countries near the venue. I always find these helpful to do some filming at, because you then don't need to take a whole crew and book expensive accommodation. It is more guerrilla-style, but very efficient and disciplined.

In 2016, the tour was to Lebanon. I have always counted it a privilege to be able to film in areas that are mentioned in the Bible. When we produce the films or TV programmes, it helps the Bible come alive in people's minds. It's no longer just a place name in a long list. They can also see what has happened to it through the centuries and the present state of that location, meeting people from the area.

I took the tour that showed us places such as Byblos and, most interesting for me, the wonderful cedars of Lebanon. I must say that most often when you actually see current sites or biblical places, there's a bit of a let-down. Today's reality is not quite as imagined when reading the Bible. The combination of tourist shops and the hustle and bustle of the place does not give you the authentic feel. The location of the cedars of Lebanon, however, *does* give you that feel. It is awesome and takes your breath away. What is still standing is only one small portion of what it must have been like to see whole hillsides covered for miles with the aromatic and beautiful trees. There was talk on the tour of not seeing this place, but I found enough support to say that we would rather spend a Sunday morning there than in a religious ceremony in a cathedral. It was a very inspiring time. The location also gave opportunities for prayer, reflection and conversation about the Temple, Solomon, and many other biblical topics.

To me, the most touching and heart-breaking part was our chance to actually spend time with refugees on the dangerous border with Syria. The Christian Church in the area has been helping these men, women and children, almost all Muslim, as they have been there for years. They were admitted, we were told, into Lebanon as refugees, but their visas had long run out. Now, years later, they could not afford the $1,000-plus cost of obtaining another visa. Thus they were in a very dangerous predicament.

I have never met such lovely and giving people as these refugees, literally without a home. Their place of residence sits on farmland that they must *rent* from the local farmer. It consists of cardboard walls covered in plastic. Ironically, as is often the case in the Middle East, a satellite dish sits on top of the ramshackle edifice, and a TV is one of the few things that they brought from their homeland!

We were offered some delicious tea, and enough cups were found for the few of us to spend more quality time sitting with them and getting to know the reality of their dire circumstances.

In some ways they were living in a great environment, but

in other ways a most miserable situation. Here they had a new chance of life away (though not that far) from the war. Yet the instability of their visa status must have weighed upon them heavily. I can now truthfully say that I probably possess more knowledge about Syrian refugees than just about every delegate at the United Nations. This is a sad situation that I find myself in regarding many areas – North Korea, for example. After spending time with Canon Andrew White (sometimes called The Vicar of Baghdad), I grew to understand that he is one of the most knowledgeable people in the world about Iraq and the Middle East. Yet he is almost never used as a source of wisdom or a sounding board for Western governments to decide policy. Most often policies are created by discussing the 'what does it mean for me/us as a country' rather than 'let's get a handle on the situation from those in the know'!

After the tour, I stayed on in Lebanon due to the fact that 1) I wanted to film and see more and 2) There was a two or three-day gap before I needed to fly into Ethiopia. I opted to take a tour to biblical Tyre and Sidon, in the south of the country. With just three or four of us on the minibus tour, I found it to be a great time to get to know the other tourists and to ask many questions of our tour guide.

To the Lebanese people such as our tour guide, they actually believe that Hezbollah, a known terrorist organisation, is a national liberating group that was hastily organised, as my tour guide said, 'because of the Israelis stealing one of our towns'.

I asked her point-blank: 'So do you believe that once that town is liberated then Hezbollah will disband?'

'Yes,' she replied. 'They will.'

The amount of Jewish and Israeli hatred was evident, as every negative thing about Lebanon was considered to be the fault of

Israel and the Jews.

There were a number of things from this particular trip that have, through the years since then, stuck in my mind.

Palestinian camps are not in any sense *camps*. That was a real shock to all of us on the tour. Most of the time they take the form of a group of shops and living accommodations above them. Once in a great while they *are* a compound surrounded by barbed wire. Yet that is the exception rather than the rule. You would not even know that they were Palestinian camps unless you were told, because they just seem like a rundown area surrounding some commerce. The news media has tended to exaggerate the conditions and the situation by never showing video of the actual camps, but groups of refugees in different situations.

The more we travelled into southern Lebanon the more we began to see three types of flags being flown. The first was the Hezbollah flag, praising the group for their massive terror inflicted on Israel. The second was a flag for martyrdom – aka suicide bombers. The third was in honour of bombings accomplished. I attempted to confirm this on the internet, but because no one seems to go into these areas, I could not do that. When you go past a graveyard you would see quite often the black flags showing that the suicide bomber, or, as they call them, martyrs, are buried there. Along the side of the roads in that part of the world you would also see large billboard-sized photographs of suicide bombers. It was very sad to see the lives of boys and girls, children and adults so taken up with murdering innocent people by suicide.

In the gift shops throughout the area you could buy Hezbollah scarves and Hezbollah purses. One man, a Canadian if I remember, purchased one even after I warned him that immigration might treat as suspicious anyone owning a Hezbollah purse!

CHAPTER 12
Country 3 – Ethiopia
(2016)

The spirit of Christ is the spirit of missions. The nearer we get to
> Him, the more intensely missionary we become.
> (Henry Martyn, missionary to India and Persia)

A woman contacted me on social media – or it could have been
via email. She visits Ethiopia each year and she thought that we
might want to do some leadership training there to help the
churches.

There are a few countries that I have often thought that if the
right invitation came along, I would accept it. Ethiopia was one of
those countries. There are so many fascinating aspects to it that
I was hoping to explore further. The Queen of Sheba returned
there from visiting King Solomon, and tradition says that the
gift he gave her was a child! Thus outside of Israel, Ethiopia has
the largest and oldest population of Jews and Jewish history. In
fact, there is a church in one of the furthest parts of Ethiopia that
is said to contain the Ark of the Covenant. Both Ethiopia and
Kenya have interested me for their African culture, history and
longevity.

Thus began a series of emails back and forth with one of the
key leaders in the Brethren movement in Ethiopia. Brethren
churches are, on the whole, quite closed, so getting an *in* with

them means that you have an opportunity to help train some leaders and youth that normally do not get outside assistance in this way.

The line at the airport to gain a visa was quite long. Although I have been in and out of Africa through the decades, it is still a bit of a culture shock dealing with African bureaucracy. Ethiopia was no exception. Eventually I was able to pay the steep fee and collect my luggage.

My host, the key leader, was young in appearance and quite exuberant. He had offered for me to stay and sleep at the offices, but I always find it better and easier to find my own accommodation, due to the fact that I like to be relaxed after speaking for hours and days on end. If sleeping and preparing and studying is also a pressure, the end results can be disastrous, and not what God could have accomplished.

The first thing that I noticed about Addis Ababa was that quite often the roads were not complete, but parts of roads. In other countries there would have been detours and warning cones. Here you feared for your life (and that of your car!) on almost every street. Because of the potholes, which I would call pot-canyons, there was often no left or right side of the street. You drove where the least amount of damage could be done to your vehicle!

I like to spend my first day in a new country or city wandering around the shops buying juices and fluids for my time there, as I mentioned earlier. I also took time to glance around my hotel. It was exactly what I look for – quiet, set back from the business of the streets, and enclosed within its own oasis. The theme seemed to be of an African compound and I fell in love with the décor and African handcrafts and paintings dotted throughout. I always enjoyed exchanging greetings with the security guard and the attendant on the desk.

There was heavy rain and often through the night one discovered certain African eccentricities. After the first day or so I would be able to predict a few minutes ahead when the power was going to go out – for minutes or hours. In my travels I have built up a small arsenal of torches and other things for such eventualities. One item I used quite extensively there was a little pyramid-shaped light that is placed into a water or other drinking bottle. It gives the room a night-light sort of glow. It was a real life-saver in Ethiopia.

Another things that I enjoy in other countries, as I have said before, is going through the TV channels to understand the culture. Here in Ethiopia there were some Christian channels but a great many Muslim channels. One night, I awoke with a start and for some reason turned on the TV – to a Japanese network. There was my Chinese designer friend and her husband on a special film about their lives! That was totally unexpected.

I also tried watching the SAT-7 children's programmes. One of them was a programme that I had watched them film at their studios in Beirut – I had been photographed with the presenters! It was a real treat to see it *in action* thousands of miles away in Africa!

Sunday morning came quickly and I was whisked away for my first preach at a very large and comparatively modern church on the edge of Addis Ababa. I had felt led of the Lord to do a series of teachings – not the same one over and over – on Psalm 23. Before I left the UK, though, I had wondered about the possibility of no one in Ethiopia being familiar with shepherding. Just before arriving at the first church and throughout the stay, I was constantly bombarded with the sight of shepherds tending their sheep. It was more than I had seen in any country that I have ever visited! I knew then that they could identify readily with the life of the shepherd.

A typical African service will last for hours. As I was preaching at a few churches, we would arrive just after the music portion and in time for the ministry of the Word of God. I would then be whisked away for the next service. For two Sundays I was privileged to share in a number of churches. One church was in the middle of nowhere with no electricity. The only light was what shone brightly in from the outside! In each church I witnessed the joy of the Lord and the praise and worship of what would more be seen in a Pentecostal church than a Brethren church!

Sandwiched in my week was my training for pastors. I had felt led by God to break the day's training up. One was theological – sharing on the Trinity. Another was a series of teachings and workshops on the problems that pastors generally face and often lead to their failure and/or downfall. As is quite common throughout the world, getting other denominational churches to cooperate is quite an achievement. I was told that after the first year there would be more churches cooperating, but I have not yet been back to take them up on that offer.

It is quite common in African countries for the visiting speaker not only to pay for their own travel arrangements, which we are used to, but also for the food and accommodation of all of the delegates attending. For a ministry such as ours, working totally by faith, that was quite an undertaking. Sadly we had to borrow the funds, with interest, to be able to pay for that.

One of the most difficult things that I find in ministry is getting people to not be moved by what I call goosebumps but by seeing the vision of what is about to be or is being accomplished. In the US there are entire companies that design financial appeal letters for the larger ministries, as I hinted at earlier. They are able to pinpoint particular buzzwords and emotion-inducing catchphrases with great accuracy and know exactly how much will be raised by each letter. It is big business.

I have often prayed for someone to come on board who is a fundraiser who, with genuine love and compassion instead of gimmicks, would be able to elicit funds from, as the Bible says in 2 Corinthians 9:7, cheerful givers. As I have had the opportunity to work with some of the biggest names in ministry I have often been grieved by the amount of manipulation that goes on in the name of God. I have even been further grieved by the waste and selfish splurges of many large ministries. One ministry I know of announced that they needed an amount in the tens of millions of dollars to reach every person on earth. At the same time (coincidentally?) the head of the ministry and his wife quietly started building a new house for the two of them costing the exact same amount of money!

I would love to be able to take on projects for our ministry in places like Ethiopia, more projects which we have been offered in North Korea, Vietnam, Cambodia, the Philippines and other places. We have tremendous open doors but need to constantly think and pray and strategise ways of finding income. People often tell me, 'God provides.' My answer to that always is, 'Yes, but He always uses people. He is not a counterfeiter making money in heaven!'

I was pleased and thrilled to see the lights switch on in people's hearts and minds as I showed them old truths in a new and more unique way. I knew that I was training a whole denomination and generation. I often attempt to fast when I am teaching. I find that the more I share God's Word the more that I need to draw on His supernatural ability and power. Fasting helps me to tap into that. The second reason is that in my desire not to insult, I might be forced to eat things that I would not normally eat. Ethiopian food is known to be unique and famous all over Africa. I can well remember being in Paris and eating at an Ethiopian restaurant and being the most ill that I have ever been in my life. This all weighed heavily on my mind, as I did not want to have a heavy schedule and be running back and forth to the toilets.

Before eating, generally someone brings a basin and a pitcher of water. The tradition is for the waiter/a servant to pour the water over your hands while you rub your hands together – soapless. They then offer you a towel to dry your rinsed hands. Instead of a separate plate, the Ethiopian way is to use a purple type of pancake as a plate. On top of this is piled all sorts of delicacies. Then another pancake is used instead of a spoon or fork. I did try it while there, but I cannot truly say that it is one of my favourites. When not fasting I traditionally like to have something simple such as a bowl of soup. This did not seem to go down well in Ethiopia with my hosts, as they were able to put away more food than I would normally eat over three days!

After a few of the Sunday meetings, we found ourselves in a part of Ethiopia that seemed to be the desert. What a glorious sight as we moved about from one location to another, seeing God's handiwork and man's design. I can remember seeing a herd of camels. Having my phone camera, I filmed them. We then heard a knock on the window from the owner of the camels, begging for funds for my 'production'!

Following the three days of pastoral training, we had all-day Saturday youth training meetings. This was another great opportunity to be able to pour into the future leaders of Ethiopia. Having ministered in youth work for many years, I could see the different types of personalities and interests. One young man, I could tell, was there at his parents' command. He was looking at his phone (it always amazes me that almost all impoverished parts of the world seem to have access to phone contracts and the internet). After the first hour and a break, he scampered off and was not seen again! A couple of others were of a similar mind, but were able to be coaxed to stick it out for the duration of the training sessions.

What really starts my engine, so to speak, are the ones that are hungry and thirsty. With my spiritual eyes, I can see them in the future going for the most difficult churches or locations, bringing in those from the wayside to have their life changed by Jesus Christ. The others that I am drawn to are those who rebel, but in a way that you can tell that the rebellion can be turned into victory as they look to God and stand against sin. I almost seek these out because they end up being the Franklin Grahams of the world. (Franklin Graham was the rebellious son of world-famous evangelist Billy Graham who has taken up the mantle of his father's ministry, along with a large humanitarian work.)

Sad to say I did not get to see the Addis Ababa that I had wanted to film. Public transport consists of thousands of minivans with someone yelling their next destination out of the window. Thankfully, someone drove me everywhere. I cannot ever remember seeing a typical taxi. On top of that, I think that I was never able to get my head around the layout of the city and country. I always try to do this on my first day in a new country – get my bearings, form my understanding of what makes them tick and how they get from point A to point B! I pity anyone renting a car and trying to access places there.

One day we went to a lovely restaurant which had been a very stylish governmental house, and it gave me a view of how the other half lives in Addis Ababa. Another sight we saw was from a restaurant atop what I believe was the tallest building in the city. It was amazing to see that hubbub from above it all.

Another thing worth noting is that in hindsight, it could possibly have been a mistake to have had my Ethiopian ministry at the tail end of a long and difficult trip. Yet schedules did not permit anything else. I always find that meeting a challenge is best at the start of a trip – this is why I try to go into North Korea ahead of a South Korean/China trip.

CHAPTER 13
The Thriller in Manila
(2016)

The most important thing as a leader
is your relationship with God.
Senator Manny Pacquiao

After a successful pastors and leaders conference in 2015 in Cambodia, the organisers, Ed and Sherry Benish, then decided to hold the next conference in the Philippines, Sherry's native country. She has always had this vision and burden to assist the pastors and leaders in her homeland. Christianity is very popular there.

When it was first announced about the next year's conference, my thought was, 'OK. Cambodia was a miracle. The Philippines would be an extraordinary miracle and most likely not to be an option for me in 2016.'

As our correspondence sped back and forth about the conference, the first thing that came to me was that I knew that there would be ministers present at the conference that were despairing and depressed about their work and ministry, and even despairing of their very life! I felt that there was at least one person who was coming to the conference that I needed to encourage away from leaving everything behind. My message would be, 'Don't Give Up!' It was that thought and seed planted inside of me that caused me to do everything I could to get there and to give that vital life-giving message to that one person, whoever they were.

As we corresponded, Sherry asked, 'Have you thought about filming an interview with Manny Pacquiao – the boxer – while you are in the Philippines?' As I very often go through the list of potential celebrities and personalities that I could interview before each trip, the name had come to me. I also followed his life and bold testimony for Jesus Christ. After retiring from boxing, Manny had become a congressman in the government. Just before the summer of 2016, he was then appointed to be a senator. He has fought many fights since I interviewed him, and he told me that since he did not take a salary from the government for his work for them, he needed to get finances to help his family, and his extended family. He also runs many charitable projects to help impoverished boys and girls.

Communications with the Philippines is often difficult. I tend to use alternative forms of telephone services – Skype, for example – which, in remote areas, tends to be very difficult. I telephoned the government offices and received what I thought was a direct telephone number for Manny. For weeks I attempted to get through. Somehow I located another number, which seemed to be a non-English-speaking home somewhere in the Philippines. My last port of call was a fax number. Since we stopped using faxes many years ago, it meant locating the old machine, hooking it up and attempting to constantly fax the senator's office. It seemed to be hopeless!

Finally, I began to consider that since Sherry had many contacts in the Philippines, she might have a contact who could fax or post a letter. Ever thoughtful and helpful, Sherry actually located someone who lived near the senator's home, and he ended up hand-delivering the letter. What a joy! I finally knew that my correspondence was with him.

Manny Pacquiao grew up in very desperate home and financial circumstances. Boxing in the Philippines was and is a way out of those struggles. To this day, Manny helps his mother and tens of thousands of needy Filipinos throughout the world.

Manny was brought up selling this and that and doing anything that would bring in money. His far from the city childhood home had the minimal of everything. Its location meant that he would climb up and down mountains to carry out the smallest errand. God, in His finite wisdom and mercy, was actually being Manny's 'trainer' and developing those muscles that he would need most in his future calling.

Manny worked his way up in the ring. Today, Manny Pacquiao is the most famous name in any Filipino's mind. His faith and his generosity is well known.

The day of my departure for the conference came and still I had no firm confirmation about the interview. But I now had some direct links with the people around him (there are dozens who help to manage the huge number of works and foundations which Manny has set up).

As I went to the airport, I had all these things rolling around in my mind – my vital talk about not giving up, which I believed would be a life-or-death presentation to at least one person, the interview, the unusual aspects of Manila that I believed that I would find myself in, and my attempt to try out a new airline that I had heard good reports of. I tend to favour one airline and get Air Miles and good service from them. However, as my remit now centred much on the Middle East, I had attempted to build up an affiliation with this airline.

At the gate, the man from the airline came up to me and asked,

'Are you alone?' 'Yes', I replied.

'I would like to upgrade you to Business Class to … (my first port of call, as the airline's home base, to change planes to Manila).'

I had already seen that this particular airline had a very high standard. I was not disappointed. From take-off to landing, I was treated with the utmost care and every single courtesy in the book! The TV monitor was state of the art as well as the seat, cushions, three-course meal, every beverage imaginable, and personal attendance by what seemed like my own stewardess! God, I believe, was showing me His favour in being a servant of His calling!

Changing planes on the next flight and going into Economy Class was a bit of a culture shock but, since the flight was short, not a major problem. Anyway, Economy was still a step above with this particular airline.

I was to be met in Manila at the airport by a man from one of the conference's sponsoring churches. I turned on my phone and found that it seemed to be out of order. In Japan I had also found the phone system to be so completely different that I was without this great convenience. After buying a Filipino SIM card and trying all sorts of contact numbers and messages and texts and emails, my driver finally showed up. We then proceeded to wait for an hour or more for a taxi! The short journey, being at Manila rush hour, took a number of hours. My weariness and jet lag was starting to set in.

I had booked a hotel away from the hustle and bustle of Manila, as I have always found that I need to prepare myself spiritually, physically and mentally before the long hours and demands of a major conference. However, my host felt that I would do better if I was at a (half-star?) hotel in a shopping mall nearer to their church (which I never saw).

In the midst of all of this, I had been able to contact one of the senator's assistants, who put me in touch with another. They told me that the senator was too busy and would not be able to have time for a TV interview. After much pleading and explaining that I had come all the way from London, I was then told to phone back in the morning and the interview would be on!

Now full of jet lag and totally exhausted – knowing that this would be my last full night of sleep for a while – I fell into a very sound sleep. Then, at midnight, there was a knock on my door. 'I have someone who wants to see you,' I was told.

Trying to wear reasonable clothing and not pyjamas, I stumbled to reception. There was my friend, a fellow speaker from the Cambodia conference. You can well imagine that in travelling you often do not remember, in the middle of the night, what country you're in or even what continent you're on. Bleary-eyed, I tried to be hospitable, eventually remembering where I was.

'I hear you're going to interview Manny Pacquiao in the morning. Can I come along?' he asked.

'OK. You can be my assistant. I always need assistants.' I then stumbled back to bed.

It was 10am and I phoned one of Manny's assistants. To me, the Filipino accent is quite difficult to get a hold of at first. It seems to be a mixture of English, Pinglish, Spanish and something else. So when I was given the address I needed help – a number of times – to get it written into English and into Filipino. Not knowing where the location was, my *assistant* and I took a taxi to that area – quite a distance from our hotel, but right near where I was originally scheduled to stay! As we said later, if I had stayed there, then my friend would not have hooked up with me and we would not have been together for the time at Manny's.

Manila is an interesting place for transport. When we showed the address of where we were headed to the Tuk Tuk driver, he loaded us both into his vehicle. My friend and I are about the same weight – about 100kg-plus-plus! I had to take a photo of us tucked into this tiny seat on a bicycle contraption, with the name of it (they all have pet names) emblazoned for all to see: *Baby!* After five minutes, he took us to another, larger, vehicle – a car taxi – and we were off.

Due to crime, political sensitivities, his position in government and his fame, Manny lives in a gated community with other well-known dignitaries and famous celebrities. I never told the taxi driver where we were going, for security reasons – just the address. When the guard on the gate asked me who we were coming to see and I said the name *Manny Pacquaio*, the taxi driver's eyes lit up like a Christmas tree and his smile reached from ear to ear. I could just imagine him going home and telling his wife whose house he had driven some passengers to! Manny is that loved and famous in the Philippines. The guard told us that we were too early and to come back later.

My friend and I had a relaxing lunch at some type of Asian restaurant, and it was well-needed. It gave us a chance to catch up and to plan the strategy for the interview, something I enjoy doing, so I am not going into a meeting cold, in spite of having done months of background research – and, in Manny's case, the reading of three books about his life, and watching a film about him.

Eventually the time came and we walked to the guard shack. They telephoned Manny's house and were told, 'He's gone out. Sorry. It's cancelled.' I immediately telephoned his assistant, who had a chat with the guard. Moments later he was 'sir'ing and apologetic and giving us directions as to where to walk.

I knew right away which house was the senator's. Even though he lived among important ambassadors, Manny's house was the one with dozens of heavily armed guards at the gate and inside the gate.

Although I have interviewed hundreds of people in my years, stepping up to the front door of one of the most beautiful homes I have ever seen was a real privilege. We were ushered into Manny's private study. Of course, we were like two kids in a candy store, taking photos of everything and us standing next to everything – including his desk nameplate!

After some time, we were ushered into Manny's dining room – a beautiful room with the largest dining table I have ever seen. All Manny's staff are treated as family, so there is a constant to-ing and fro-ing and meals being cooked. I was introduced to a Christian Broadcasting Network (CBN) crew and got to chat to them about their upcoming interview with Manny for a special charity presentation.

Sitting down with everyone at a Filipino meal is like being in a sumptuous banquet. All of the food was new to me, and I had my favourites! The huge table was actually full of all of us enjoying fellowship and food together. Overlooking the beautiful home of the senator, its pool, gardens and even into the living room across the way, was a real treat! Like Manny himself, everything is open.

Eventually the senator came into the room. When I interview Christians and Christian leaders, I always pray for them just after we take some press photos and before the interview itself.

After prayer with the senator, we had a great thirty-minute interview about boxing, potential matches, his family, his work as a senator, his testimony and his future. Then we stayed around and chatted for another hour or two and prayed again for him and for his family. The entire experience was one of the most outstanding in my life. We have stayed in touch, which is a privilege.

He excused himself and we packed up the equipment. On the way out, we decided to take some photos of him playing chess back in his office and this led to another half-hour of fellowship and chat. As our taxi pulled up and we drove away, it was just another great praise and joy-fest over God's marvellous grace and work to bring us to meet and interview such a great servant of God.

In the early hours of the next morning, our alarms rang on our phones and we rushed downstairs to go to what we thought would be a bus ride to the conference location. Instead it was another tiny Tuk Tuk with our bags loaded onto a third Tuk Tuk with each of us going – somewhere.

So we arrived at the meeting point of the coaches! It was 3am and we were in front of a closed McDonald's! About 100 to 150 of us in the dark... Some people recognised me from the Cambodia conference. One couple took me aside and asked me to pray for them – then and there – for them to have a baby as they were told that they were barren. What a joy that was! After a few more requests for personal prayer we were bundled into a series of buses for the three hours-plus to the conference centre!

Tucked tightly together on a bumpy bus was quite an experience. What a joy to pray over and see this wonderful nation for hundreds of miles – with a few pit stops along the way. Finally, we arrived at the conference centre. We had dormitory-style rooms with two bunk beds and a trundle bed that slipped out from under the bottom bunk.

The three-day conference was packed, from 5 to 6am until way past midnight.

The weather was quite unsettled. The meeting area seated over 1,000 with a metal roof and open sides. It was full to capacity. My turn came to speak on the important subject of 'Don't Give Up!'. I felt the anointing of God so strongly as I stood up. Yet, as I began to share God's Word, the most torrential downpour of heavy rain started to pelt the metal roof, causing unbearable noise and disruption. The louder I spoke, the heavier the rain became. Yet, I did not stop as I recognised it as the work of the enemy, and gave the powerful message. I had people close their eyes and I asked who it was that I had been sent to the Philippines to share this message with. One hand went up – my time and energy was well worth it! But then another hand, and another. At the end, I found that there were twelve people who had despaired of life and ministry and were considering ending their lives. Afterwards, one of the speakers told me privately that it was also a message for him, but he did not want to raise his hand – because he was a speaker! What joy filled my heart; the whole trip had been worthwhile.

On the second night I was sharing on the subject of the Jewish background to what we call the Lord's Supper – actually, the Passover service. Afterwards, a number of pastors said that they were going to revamp their entire communion service to include the actual symbolism which is lost without the Passover context. The same weather experience happened again as I prepared to stand up to share God's Word. The sun had been out. The skies were blue. Yet as I stood up, they darkened and it started to rain. Then it began to pelt down – these were the only times during the entire conference that this happened with such ferocity. People's eyes were as large as saucers as they understood the significance of me speaking twice and the same weather phenomena happening at that exact moment.

As I shared, my voice was even starting to give out because of the volume and force that I was having to use to be audible. Now, besides the heavy rain, there was thunder and lightning.

'I don't care what you try to throw at us, Satan, *I will get this message out!*' I yelled. I had heard and read about these things happening, but here I was in the midst of a spiritual challenge!

People started looking around and began crying and putting their hands up. They understood that often in life we come against a challenge – the forces of God against the forces of Satan! This seemed to be one of them.

Afterwards, throughout the conference, people were remarking about the messages and the challenge against God's Word during my messages and the victory in Jesus Christ. It was a very special privilege to, again, be able to impact the leaders of another nation and see them encouraged.

As we all travelled back to Manila after the conference it was a joy to see some of the areas that we dropped people off at. In the previous year's conference we had discovered that about 50 per cent of the pastors and leaders were actually homeless. It has touched my heart to know of the faithfulness of these men and women of God, who keep on, in spite of external circumstances, strengthening God's people and helping them to grow in the Faith.

CHAPTER 14
My Film of Living Jewishly
(2017)

I've started to look at life differently. When you're thanking
God for every little you – every meal, every time you wake up,
every time you take a sip of water – you can't help but be more
thankful for life itself, for the unlikely and miraculous fact that
you exist at all.

(A.J. Jacobs, https://www.goodreads.com/quotes/230131-i-ve-
started-to-look-at-life-differently-when-you-re-thanking)

When you are filming, almost every week you tend to start
running into familiar faces. I first met D on an East End of London
gangster film and we had a chance to chat quite in depth. When I
found out that he was Jewish and had been an Israeli soldier and
that he had lived in Israel for over a decade, my interest piqued.
I have, so far, visited the nation a total of seven times, as well as
leading tours there. I told him many of the things that I loved
about the country and the people, and he did the same. I shared
with him how that as a Christian believer in *his* Messiah, Yeshua,
I have, all of my life, taught about the Jewish background to the
Christian faith. He seemed quite impressed.

We next met on a Pierce Brosnan film. One of the first
things D shared with me as we got reacquainted was that a
big Jewish film was about to be produced in London and that

they wanted all Jewish people in it. He told me to mention his name, as he was portraying a rabbi. He also told me the name of his agency and said that I should give it a try. I wrote the longest possible pleading letter, explaining that although maybe not a Jew outwardly, I was circumcised in the heart. I told the agency about all of my Jewish connections, trips to Israel and knowledge and interests. After pressing 'Send' it took a mere three minutes before I received an email back, saying that they were putting me forward for the film!

In filming you just never know, often until the last minute, whether or not you are merely pencilled in or whether you have a firm booking. I was still pencilled in, but given a costume-fitting date. That date was changed a number of times. Finally, I was confirmed for that shoot. What happiness that was, as I knew that it was going to not just be a dramatic feature film, but also provide a great deal of teaching about the Hebrew Scriptures.

It was finally decided that rather than have a separate costume-fitting day (which also means a bit of funding to cover travel), it would take place on the day of the shoot. That means rather than knowing exactly what you are going to be wearing, it would be necessary to bring everything you have that would potentially fit the bill. I had earlier taken a photograph with some of my Jewish religious items on, including a copy of the *Tanakh* in my hand. My suitcase was packed.

In location filming, you have both a location and a base. Base is where background artists and some crew wait until called on the set – or the location. I arrived on a drizzly day in a part of London and found, before 7am, the location at a social club. Inside was a hub of activity. Lighted mirrors were scattered throughout the room, and photographs of a large collection of mostly Orthodox males and a few females at each mirror. One area, more like the

Tabernacle with its cloth walls, was reserved for wardrobe – one for males and one for females. Hair and make-up were done at the same mirrors. The continual call came out: 'If you have been to wardrobe and make-up, please go out to the food wagon and have breakfast.' I had been to neither.

Eventually I was called into wardrobe. We had been told that the scene was of a Jewish funeral. I had specifically gone to Golders Green, the large, mostly Jewish area of London, to make sure that I had a *kippah* (skull cap) that would be appropriate to a Jewish funeral. For a few pounds I bought a nice black one. In Israel I had bought a number of items including a few *kippahs*, but was unable to locate them. I took the time to explore much of Golders Green, my first visit there, buying some delicious bagels and a few pastries, immersing myself in the culture. Directly across from the bagel shop I discovered a place that I have since returned to a number of times. It is a second-hand shop that has a number of Jewish items for a fraction of the price in the main Jewish stores. I bought a second black *kippah* and a number of other items, again to immerse myself in Judaica – both because of the role and also because of my love for the Jews and Israel.

As I opened my suitcase in the wardrobe department at base, I was asked by the costume assistant if I was Jewish. 'Pretty close,' was my response. I then proceeded to unpack all of my items – *Tanakh*, a selection of about five *kippahs*, two kinds of prayer shawls with the prayer tassels.

As I showed the wardrobe man everything I had, he questioned me, 'Are you sure that you are not Jewish?'

I said, 'Well, maybe on my Father's side!'

Later when I tried this line out, I was corrected. Judaism comes from the mother's side and it is this side of the family that establishes Jewish identity. A fact that I had forgotten through the years.

'Do you have anything brighter?' I was asked.

'Well, I thought I was going to a funeral, so brought everything black or with black shading,' I replied.

'Do you have anything without button-down collars?' I was asked. I did not. So wardrobe gave me a blue tie, a white shirt without a button-down collar, a grey cardigan, and the rest was all my own costume.

All dressed, I was then sent to make-up, where my *kippah* was fastened to the back of my head. I was now set to go.

There was a great discussion at breakfast and I began to learn of the plight of twenty-first-century Jews. For some reason the caterer, in spite of there being an almost 100 per cent Jewish cast, had cooked bacon and sausages. Later in the day, I was doubled over in laughter as a rabbi showed me what I jokingly called 'Jewish porn'. It was a photo of him seemingly having a piece of bacon in his mouth! Most of the Jews around thought that that was hilarious.

My friend D was in disbelief that, instead of a strictly *kosher* food offering, there would be such insensitivity. I had been emailed asking whether or not I required a *kosher* lunch and I had replied to the affirmative. It was that that really opened doors with people to explain my beliefs and faith.

Eventually our time came to ride the minibus to the location, seemingly about five miles away through London traffic. As we approached the synagogue, I noticed what I have noticed around all synagogues and Jewish educational institutions in Britain – very high security. In this case there was the security of a large big-budget Hollywood-style film as well as the security of a Jewish location *and* the need to stop anyone from bringing any non-*kosher* food into the building. Our bags were checked through on a table, a security wristband given, and then our bags rechecked at the gates.

The synagogue had a history dating back hundreds of years, and we were sent to the activity centre. It was lined with beautiful historical paintings of many of the leaders of the synagogue. As Jewish families were forced to flee persecution in Amsterdam, they set up this community in London which, eventually, led to the building of a very ornate and beautiful synagogue.

At base I had noticed bags of brown wigs which were placed on the women. In Judaism it is believed to be immodest if a woman's head is not covered. One can see the streets of Golders Green filled with women with almost the exact same style and colour of wig. Interestingly, a national newspaper had photographed the action on one of the days of filming at Golders Green and had remarked that the lead actress (who was also the producer of the film) had her hair done up modestly and it was brown. It was actually the wig, but this must have been written by an unknowing reporter.

After many hours we were led to the actual set – the inside of the synagogue. In my younger years I used to teach, in each of my church plants, about Jewish manners and customs. This helped people to understand more deeply what was behind much of the writing of the New Testament. For example, one cannot understand the Lord's Supper (communion) without understanding the Passover. When Jesus talked about 'this cup', He was differentiating it from the other cups at the Passover. When He talked about 'this bread', He was also differentiating it from the other two slices of unleavened bread at the Passover. It is all so symbolic.

I was chatting with everyone that I could and sharing with them about how beautiful the different aspects of the synagogue were. The eternal light as a picture of God's eternal presence. The central podium or, as it is called, the *bema* is what is talked about when the New Testament refers to the *bema* seat or judgement seat of Christ. In some of the older Jews present, my words seemed to bring back memories of things that they had been taught in their youth. Within the ark stood the scrolls – the Word of God. They are touched only with a silver utensil so as not to desecrate it or stain it, as they are made with animal skins.

Years ago I asked a rabbi why there was not a shortage of scrolls – them being so difficult to produce by hand and on animal skin. (There are also no chapter and verse headings; one has to memorise the Hebrew Scriptures to find the place.) I was told that in actual fact there is a surplus of scrolls. Incredulous, I asked, 'How can that be?'

The answer, I was told, was that Hitler, when he burned hundreds of synagogues, kept the scrolls. His plan was to make a giant bonfire and destroy the Word of God forever. Hitler died before being able to accomplish this horrific vision. Thus, what he attempted to do actually led to the reverse – a surplus of the Word of God!

The plotline of the film that I was appearing in was about a very old rabbi who was preaching and then died mid-sentence. As is done in the wisdom of Hollywood, the first day we were holding the funeral and the celebration of the life of the rabbi. The second day we had his actual death.

The funeral was Judaism in all of its finest. Each of the fifty to 100 of us 'rabbis' all had our prayer shawls. Most had the black tall hats over their *kippahs*. As many of the men were genuine Jews, they also had the marvellous characteristic scraggly beards.

Another story that I shared with many of the Jews who would listen to me was about a book once popular at airports around the

English-speaking world. The book was called *The Year of Living Biblically*. (This is about to be turned into a major TV series in America.) I found the book fascinating. The author, A.J. Jacobs, took a year out to learn the encyclopaedia and became what he called a 'Know it all'. This particular year he took out to live the Bible. Because of the breakdown of the Old and New Testaments, he spent nine months living Judaism to its fullest and the Old Testament, and then three months living the Christian life and New Testament. Along the way he questioned all of the reasons behinds biblical laws and sayings and getting input from the whole spectrum of Judaism and Christianity.

I often tell the story about his long-suffering wife. AJ (a man I have come to know as we have corresponded back and forth for years) plunged in at the deep end. Everything in the Old Testament, he did. He wore linen garments and refused to shave, as commanded. He refused to sit on the Underground as a woman might have been menstruating and thus would make him unclean. So he *never* sat on a seat where a woman had sat.

One day his wife had had enough. When he came home bedraggled and tired, he went to sit down in his favourite chair. She told him that he had better not sit there because she sat there. Indeed, she had sat on every seat in the whole house. This put him in a quandary which he had to work out!

I found this to be the most helpful book outside of the Bible to teach me about what the Bible is all about, and the reasons behind many Old Testament laws and practices. AJ started as an atheist and, through this one year, became more of what he described as a sympathetic agnostic – almost a believer! Years later when interviewing the Queen's and parliament's chaplain Rose Hudson-Wilkin, I asked her the question I have asked many others – 'What book are you reading at the moment?' She told me that her favourite book was *The Year of Living Biblically*. After the interview I told her that I knew AJ and that he promised I could interview him one day. She asked if she could carry my camera so she could be in on that interview! I told AJ about this and he was so excited, as his wife is very interested in royal things.

The gist of the two days of filming was that after the elder rabbi died, they had appointed a younger one who felt inadequate to take the reins of such a heavy responsibility. I found the discussions and sermons in the film to be quite enlightening as to understanding more of the Bible and how some Jews think about life and the Bible.

In the course of a couple of days of filming, I was able to chat with probably about 100 Jews. Of those I had in-depth discussions with about twenty. Towards the end of the first day, a man who, obviously, had been listening in on my discussions with others, came up to me.

'I am a Jew and I believe in Jesus.'

His boldness and directness shocked me. Knowing that we were at the end of the day, I released a barrage of things about Jesus – Yeshua – and His Jewishness. I shared about how when the woman with the issue of blood (see Luke 8) wanted to touch the hem of Jesus' garment it was not the hem that she wanted to touch, but the tassels. The man knew full well that the tassels stood for the promises of the Word of God. I pointed to the fake tassels that we wore instead of an under prayer shawl with them on.

'She understood the power of the Word of God,' I explained. I gave him my card and he went away with much to think about. When lunchtime approached, the people who had not ordered kosher meals were asked to board the minibuses to go back to base for a non-kosher lunch. To my surprise, all but twenty of us left. I looked around in disbelief.

'What is this about?' I asked D and a woman he was talking with. Sadly they explained that this was the problem of Jewish manners and practice in the twenty-first century. People may be Jews by blood, but not so much now by practice.

Because of the Bible verse that says not to boil a kid (goat) in its mother's milk (see Exodus 23:19), rabbinical scholars have decided that milk and meat can never be combined. There are two kitchens where the two never meet. I have had delicious meals in Israel with meat and have it followed by very tasty ice cream, only to discover that it is actually non-dairy because of the requirement.

In my discussions that lunchtime, I also mentioned about the most delicious ribs/pork in the world, found in Israel. D, knowing Israel, knew the *kibbutz* that I was talking about. Because the rabbinical law forbids the feet of a pig from touching the holy ground of the Holy Land, this *kibbutz* has pallets for the pigs to walk on so that they can have a great delicacy for non-Jews and, at the same time, keep the law.

Kibbutzim in Israel date back to the early days of the formation of modern Israel. They are more like communes and usually specialise in one particular item that will help bring in income. I told D and the Jewish woman that the most delicious ice cream that I ever had was in the Negev desert on a *kibbutz* that is most famous for its dairy herd. Again, D knew exactly which one I was talking about. The tourist site where people are baptised in the Jordan River, supposedly where Jesus was, is also on a *kibbutz*. They produce videos and photographs of the event and have a gift shop featuring everything from bottles of water from the Jordan to anointing oil.

As we finally wrapped (ended filming for the day) and headed onto the minibus – all with our *kippahs*, one man remarked,

'Be careful where you walk wearing these. You can get in deep trouble.' Sadly, that is the situation, as anti-Semitic elements seem to take hold more and more in such a once diverse city such as London.

I still continue to go to Golders Green to visit and prayer-walk through the area every couple of weeks. My love for the Jewish people and the land is a burning flame and I yearn to share with them who their Messiah really is.

CHAPTER 15
Focus on the Face of the Man on the Cross

God is still looking for the prepared spiritual leaders. He looks
for the person of the Holy Spirit, the person of prayer, the
person of dream and vision, the person of the Word of God, the
person of love, and the person of humility.
(Dr Young Hoon Lee, senior pastor, Yoido Full Gospel Church,
Seoul, South Korea)

As I write, I have just filmed a most marvellous advert for TV. It
was for a high street bank and featured a number of war veterans
that I was privileged to be among for an entire day. To hear
their stories of battles and fatalities, losses and grief, watching
many of them walking on one natural leg and one artificial, was
challenging to me.

The centre of the entire scene was a cross. We were all supposed
to look at it. The director was French, so English was not his first
language. In one of the scenes he was telling the cameraman to
have a close-up of me but his words came out, in their meaning,
a bit differently. The words that he repeated over and over were:
'Focus on the face of the man on the cross.' Of course, he meant,
'Focus on the face of the man who is looking at the cross.' His
words were so impactful to me that my eyes even started tearing-
up as he said it louder and louder. As I was thinking about

completing this book, that phrase rang louder and louder in my ears and in my heart. I realised that that is what I aim and strive towards doing – getting people to look at the face of the man on the cross!

We too often focus on the victory of Jesus Christ, which is tremendous and the reason that we can become a child of God – by receiving the completed work of Jesus Christ and His victory over sin and of death. Yet, in the Roman Catholic tradition they focus on the sufferings of Jesus Christ on the cross. We, as Protestants, often bypass that. Yet I believe that I have grown more as I – like my friend who roomed with me years earlier urged me – have learned to die with Jesus and take up my cross daily. I believe that our victory comes when we realise, as I attempt to do, that we *have been crucified* with Christ. Yet we live. The life that we live is not ours. Too many Christians are waiting until heaven to live for Jesus and to focus on the important things!

We need to live and breathe Jesus, and God the Father, and the Holy Spirit! This is not a one day a week existence but a 24/7 living, breathing lifestyle. When I started praying in China for God to order my footsteps, I fully expected Him to guide me – while in China. Great things happened, as I have shared. Yet when I realised that 24/7 I can offer my life and time to Him and have Him take me to difficult places and enjoyable places – even outside of China! – mountaintops and dark valleys, then I can know the ever-present, ever-sustaining, ever-growing fellowship of my Creator God with me, a 'dead pilgrim'!

I find people are encouraged by the stories of my life that I share, but only if those stories are sewn together with what it is all about. I am not some frequent traveller and flier going from one jolly to another. I am an ambassador for Jesus Christ who does not know when or where his next assignment is! I can see that God has strung together my life, like Corrie ten Boom says, in a series of seemingly unconnected events and footsteps. Yet, looking back, I can see that for much of my life I was a signpost pointing people to Jesus!

Living such a life I often get criticised for bragging. But I am not bragging! My point is that in spite of me, in spite of my shortcomings and sin, in spite of my not looking the part or having the proper connections or enough financing, God can use me.

I believe that that fact and this book will encourage you as it has encouraged me. God seldom uses an apostle Paul, full of the right credentials. He uses a shepherd boy, an adulterer, a murderer, a loser, and turns each life around – if we allow Him to! So many feel that they are too bad for Jesus to save them. The tragedy I find is when people think that they are too good to need salvation. Their own righteousness, they believe, is enough. But it is not!

The Old Testament Law was used, I believe, to show that humanity cannot keep the law by themselves. It takes the power of God to live and breathe God's Word. We are His living Bible! We are living epistles; He is written on our hearts for others to read.

My life is not over. Great men and women of God were used greatly when they thought that it was time to relax! God even made Abraham a dad at the age of great-great-grandpas.

We must see ourselves as pilgrims, *not* settlers, on this road of life. We are striving, moving, progressing to be more and more like Jesus every day, if we allow His Spirit to show us the areas that He needs to work on. Like a piece of stone in the mighty hands of a great sculptor, He needs to knock off chunks of me so that He can be seen in and through me.

I envision looking from eternity to people whose lives I touched by some word, a testimony of God's faithfulness, or some kind act which was a message directing them to focus on the man on the cross. That is my ambition, my goal – to be a ragged signpost showing the way to Jesus, to heaven and to eternal life.

CONTACTS – STAY IN TOUCH

Book website:
info@progressofamodernpilgrim.com
www.progressofamodernpilgrim.com

Our Christian programming:
www.principles.tv
info@principles.tv

Our 'inspirational' programming:
www.principlestvgroup.com
info@principlestvgroup.com

Our production website:
www.onlocationinternational.com
info@onlocationinternational.com

Our humanitarian work:
www.handsglobal.org
info@handsglobal.org

For Principles TV Tours to the Bible Lands:
http://principlestv.webs.com/tour-bible-lands

Our Principles TV Youtube Channel – Christian programming:
https://www.youtube.com/channel/
UCfNUvmzjXfQgP9al3cjmgfw

Our Principles TV Group – 'inspirational' programming:
https://www.youtube.com/channel/UCxc2VCnTS6pRxHu_
ipQRddA

Harvest Fields Commissioning International
P. O. Box 740
Hemel Hempstead
Herts
HP1 3RH
United Kingdom

A U. K. Registered Charity (Number 1099460) and a Company
Limited by Guarantee (Number 4842650).